Understand

André

About this book

"Understanding Vegans" is an intimate but globally relevant account of what it means to be a vegan in a non-vegan world. Tired of dog-loving-cow-eating twisted morals and millions of excuses for billions of victims, André Huber makes a compelling case for why it's time to rethink our view of vegans and join their cause.

André Huber is an educator and writer with a secret agenda: he wants you to go vegan (unless you are stranded on a deserted island with a pig). He has been a vegan for more than a decade.

For more content follow:

 @UnderstandingVegans

André Huber

UNDERSTANDING VEGANS

What you always wanted to know
about this one annoying friend of yours

Copyright © 2024 André Huber
All rights reserved.

Second Edition 2024
Independently published.

ISBN: 9798328388764

Although all care has been taken with advice and information, no responsibility is accepted for accuracy. A qualified health professional should be consulted for any medical advice.

To my biggest ally, *Elena.*

Chapters

Intro 1
1 What is a vegan? 11
   Definition 11
   Plant-based diets and other terms 16
   The common denominator for vegans and vegetarians 20
   What vegans are not 22
2 Preachy vegans 25
   Being vegan in a non-vegan world 27
   Early "enthusiasm" 33
   The difficulty of discussing veganism with non-vegans 41
3 I can understand vegetarian, but vegan? 47
   Vegans are extreme 48
   Reasons for being vegan 50
      Dairy 51
      Eggs 53
      Honey 56
      Fur 59
      Leather 60
      Wool & silk 62
      Feathers 64

Performing animals	65
Zoos	66
Cosmetics and pharmaceuticals	69
Need more reasons? Your health and the planet	73
4 So what DO vegans eat?	**77**
Eating out	84
What do (some) vegans (not) eat	93
5 Deserted islands, lions and avocados	**97**
If we are not supposed to eat meat, why do we have canines?	98
But lions kill to eat meat, so why shouldn't I? It's all part of the circle of life.	98
Humans have been eating meat for thousands of years!	99
I don't care about animals…	100
If you were on a deserted island, stranded with a pig, wouldn't you eat it?	101
Where do you get your protein from?	101
Avocados are bad for the environment, soybeans destroy the Amazon, vegans are killing the planet!	102
I once knew a vegan who was sick after a month and now eats meat again.	104
Plants feel pain too!	104
Eskimos need to eat meat to survive!	105
You should worry about more important things, like human suffering!	106
We can't even reach equality among humans, so what's the point of fighting for animals?	107
Humans are above animals!	108
Veganism is a luxury problem!	109

Vegans should stop forcing their minority views on others, everybody has the right to eat whatever they want. 111
We need to hunt to control animal populations! 114
Vegans need to take pills, this is not natural and therefore can't be good. 115
Our animal protection laws are already very good. In our country there's no need to worry! Just buy local! 116
My actions will not make a difference anyway 118
We all cause harm through our existence and vegans kill animals too! 120
We all just need to relax a bit more about food and enjoy life. 120
Why is all this BS so predictable? 122

6 A vegan world **125**
7 Just do it **133**
8 Counting on the next generation **143**
Sources **149**

Intro

"I could never go vegan!"…said every vegan ever before going vegan. I was no different. I grew up in a small town in Switzerland, a country in which cheese is basically the national dish. I was lucky to be raised in a household where home-cooked meals were the norm and food was never scarce, so I never felt the need to question what I was eating. I was simply a fortunate kid, not exactly a picky eater and blessed with a healthy appetite. As a teenager in high school, I went through times when burgers from the yellow arches were a staple lunch and I took pride in the fact that I was often beating my friends in juvenile eating competitions. Apart from maybe breakfast – I am a milk and cereal type of guy – I ate meat in one way or another for pretty much every meal. Life was good though and food even better: maybe ignorant bliss. It's not that I wasn't aware that the meat I was eating came from an animal or that the milk in my cereal originated from a cow. But I grew up in a world where nobody around me questioned at all whether this is something one should be concerned about and vegetarians were something one made fun of at the max. I even remember vividly eating at an all-you-can-eat restaurant specialized in chicken wings with outdoor seating, where the "theme" included freely roaming chickens in the garden. So basically, they were running around our legs while we were chewing on the legs of their relatives. This macabre setup only prompted a few bad jokes from guests, our young selves included. I guess some felt genuine pity for the birds, but it sure did not seem to spoil anybody's appetite. After all, these wings were known throughout the region and pretty damn tasty.

From early on, I loved animals. Well, not ALL animals, I have always been quite arachnophobic, but you get the idea – everything on four legs at least. Growing up as a single child, my most loyal companion was our dog, who had been around ever since I can remember. Technically, he wasn't our first pet. I have very vague memories of a pair of guinea pigs, who I would feed cucumber peel to as a small child, but apparently it took me days to realize when they no longer were around. When I was in elementary school, I made a convincing case to my parents that I wanted to have turtles and would be willing to take care of them every day. I did keep my promise, but after a few years the interest in collecting fresh leaves outside every morning waned off and we returned the turtles to the breeder, who found a new place for them. As much as I got out of the experience of taking care of animals whose well-being was my responsibility, in hindsight it is of course a painful reminder of what is happening only too often with pets: kids want them, kids no longer want them and then they end up in a shelter at best. But it was a completely different story with our family dog as he was never truly my responsibility in the first place. He was just there, part of the family, part of my normal everyday life. As he got quite old for a dog, I was blessed with many years of his company. Although I don't remember much from my life at three years old, I remember vividly the moment we chose him from a litter at a local farm and walked home as a family with a new member. But seventeen years later, the day eventually came when his health deteriorated to a point where my parents decided to release him from the struggle and pain. A date was arranged when the doctor would come to our home. I myself was not going to be present as I was away for a school camp that week. But honestly, I don't know how I would have coped with that situation in person. I was an adult on paper by that time, but also my parents deeply struggled with that moment. It is in many ways the parting of a true family member and the fact that "Bobi", as he was called, wasn't a human being did in no way mitigate the emotional pain. So when I had to leave for school camp, I knew it was the final goodbye. I was home alone with him. I gave him some dog biscuits, kissed him on the head and left the apartment. He was too busy enjoying his snack to pay too much attention to my parting, which was maybe all the better for me. I locked the door behind me and with teary eyes was off knowing this had just been the final goodbye.

Besides the pets we had, I also enjoyed observing animals in nature. Every pond was a potential treasure trove full of small life to be discovered and observed. I caught caterpillars and saw them cocooning up in my jar and turning into butterflies, I caught frogs and crabs and observed them for hours. I would go through rolls of camera film at the zoo and probably like most kids wanted to work with animals professionally at some point. Of course all my favorite cartoon characters on TV were based on animals, I cheered for Jerry not the be caught by Tom, I didn't want Bugs Bunny to get shot by Elmer Fudd, or the Road Runner to be eaten by Wile E. Coyote. I cried watching the Lion King and Dumbo, feeling just as touched by the fate of these characters as if they were human beings. I had an entire array of stuffed animals that I loved dearly and gave names to. In other words, I grew up with what may seem like an eager interest in animals. But when you think about it, it's probably nothing out of the ordinary. Many children (and adults) have pets that they love. We all grow up with sympathies for animals, whether real ones or fictional ones. None of us wanted Bambi's mother to die. So yes, like most other children and adults, I also never actively wanted to hurt animals. That seems almost like an obvious thing to say – but, well, we will get there.

In my childhood, we did not eat out very often. My mother cooked every day and we ate most of the time what I would consider fairly traditional, local cuisine. Probably the most exotic food memory that I have from my earlier childhood is a westernized version of Chinese food, but the flavors of that "Duck Sweet Sour" seemed out of this world to me. Despite or maybe because of my upbringing with rather limited exposure to dishes from other cultures,

Intro

I was always curious about foods I was not familiar with. The only food I remember seeing on other people's plates that I did not dare trying myself were snails on a holiday in France. I discovered most international cuisines only as a young adult when I had more exposure to the seemingly endless possibilities of life in a city and started to make more mature restaurant choices than the aforementioned hamburger lunches. Amidst my explorations of what foods other cultures have to offer, I one day read about a new restaurant in town that served vegan food. I was in my mid-twenties and understood that this implied food prepared without meat, milk, or eggs, but it was still I highly exotic concept in my world at the time. I was intrigued from a purely culinary point of view. I could hardly think of a dish that would have met the criteria. It seemed so limiting. "I could never go vegan!" I still remember when I said it before even trying anything at the restaurant. How did the food taste that didn't contain any of these seemingly essential ingredients? Let's say I was not very impressed. Both the burger and the brownie for dessert had a weird texture. And yet it was only a matter of months from that experience until I would start identifying myself as a vegan.

So what happened? One minute I was in the middle of gaining momentum in my culinary maturation, I read cookbooks, I started to search out more fancy food items in specialized supermarkets and was discovering the foods of the world, while the next minute I settled for what I learned was a rubbery imitation of a burger patty called

Seitan that vegans eat instead of meat? Well, quite simply put, I started seeing the world with different eyes.

It all started with a book challenging industrialized food production systems, the famous *Omnivore's Dilemma* by Michael Pollan.[1] Coincidentally, a TV station showed various documentaries surrounding the topic of food production just around the time I was finished with that book. What I saw definitely struck a nerve, the evil machinery of massive scale food production clearly did not look like something that could be good from any possible angle. Not healthy for the consumer, not healthy for the planet, and probably not a very nice experience for these thousands of cows, pigs and chickens that were shown crammed together in their short-lived experience as units on factory farms. So I turned vegan. Not. Although I understood that part of solving the problem I was presented with on TV should entail limiting especially my consumption of meat, my immediate instinct was trying to improve my meat consumption. I started to research possibilities to buy meat directly from local farms and tried to find out all I could about their "production chains", like how the animals were kept on the respective farms as well as where and how they were slaughtered. After all, if the animals had a "good life" and were slaughtered "humanely", then it would be a much more ethical purchase than the anonymous piece of meat obtained at the supermarket, which suddenly seemed an unacceptable thing to buy. I got in touch with farmers and producers to ask them questions about their practices and continued for a while with a life of more conscious consumption of meat. Until I came across a few sentences in another book that caught me a bit off-guard. They are from Karen Duve's *Anständig Essen*, a German book about ethical eating choices.[2] The following is my free translation:

> If it is not ok to mistreat animals, how can it be ok to kill them? [...] Animal welfare concerns in farming, where the goal is to kill the animal, are a contradiction in itself. I respect the needs of an animal for enough space and fresh air, make sure it has a space to sleep, the right food and throw a ball into the cage so it has something to play with, but the most basic of its needs, the will to live, I simply ignore.

My ethics changed forever. The idea resonated with me so strongly that it suddenly became very clear that I was just kidding myself all along. So I eliminated once and for all an inner conflict that I managed to suppress surprisingly well all my life: you cannot like someone or at least respect someone, wanting well for them, but then simply take their life away at your will. So that was it. After roughly 25 years of eating meat, I stopped from one day to another and I have never looked back since. Oh, and don't feel sorry for me – the food has gotten better.

So why this book? Isn't the internet full of resources about veganism? Absolutely. In fact, I would strongly encourage you to spend some time on YouTube and watch some videos that show what's going on behind the closed doors of big barns and slaughterhouses. Watch a few documentaries. I find that only moving images can fully transport the emotion of what an animal fearing for its life must be going through or the agony of physical suffering. It is too easy to look the other way, saying "I can't watch that" and then eat some chicken nuggets five minutes later. I challenge you to look into the eyes of a cow lined up for slaughter. You will find the same fear you will find in a human's eye. Put yourself in their shoes and then make your judgement about vegans' decision to not partake in such a world. But still we are few, a misunderstood minority, and I hope that by sharing my experiences as a vegan in a non-vegan world, I can give you a glimpse of what it's like from our perspective. Maybe you are thinking about going vegan yourself, maybe someone in your life has gone vegan and you hope to make sense of their decision. This book is for you then. But it is also for me. One of the most frustrating aspects of being a vegan in a non-vegan world is that people around you will want to understand your reasons, which is a hard thing to explain in a few quick sentences and without making them feel judged. Here I have the space to get all my thoughts off my chest in an organized and hopefully entertaining manner.

Do I have the audacity to speak for all vegans? Certainly not. Although the title may suggest that vegans are a homogenous group, they obviously are not. No group of people is and if you claim otherwise, you probably already have a strong bias against that group. At the same time, we do share many experiences as a group and although I cannot speak for everyone, I do believe that after having been in and around this circle for over a decade, I do have a certain understanding of these shared experiences. Nevertheless, I obviously write from the life I have been living as a vegan (singular), so read *Understanding Vegans* (plural) with that in mind.

Do I want to convert you to veganism in this book? Yes. I would be lying if I said that the ultimate goal of trying to make somebody see your perspective is not for them to share this perspective themselves eventually. I'm advertising a set of ethics and a view of the world that I believe to be a better compass for navigating our existence on this planet than the one you may (consciously, subconsciously or unconsciously) be basing some of your current decisions on. But I am not telling you what to do here. I tell you how I feel about certain things and let you draw your own conclusions for yourself. If you read this book and the next time you bump into me you don't ask me whether I would eat an animal if I was stranded on a deserted island, then it's a small victory for me. You can read the answer to that question in chapter 5.

Oh, and one final thing: Please excuse my directness. I know, the last thing the world needs right now is another self-righteous prick yelling insults at others and that is certainly not my intention. Look at it as an exclusive behind-the-scenes VIP-access to the mind of a vegan. Our daily bread for survival and sanity is the public fake smiles while suffering on the inside, so part of *Understanding Vegans* is the removal of that mask for full transparency. I really did try to stay diplomatic, I swear, but judge for yourself. It's not you, it's me. OK no, it's you and the world you live in, but it's not personal. You just happened to have picked up a book called *Understanding Vegans*, so try to understand. Thank you.

1 What is a vegan?

So what exactly is a vegan anyway, you might wonder. The first thing people usually try to figure out about you when you say that you are a vegan is where your boundaries are – like, where do you draw the line? Even with the term being more known these days you will have people asking you if you eat fish, if you can eat gluten or if you can be a bit less complicated and make an exception for once. Most of the time, food is the main focal point when people hear the term vegan. But that's exactly where misunderstandings arise because veganism is clearly more than a diet. So let's try to figure out what a "textbook-vegan" really is.

Definition

People living according to similar values as present-day vegans go back quite far in history. Vegetarianism and the opposition to killing animals go back hundreds if not thousands of years BC and already had been a topic of concern for Greek philosophers like Pythagoras and Plato.[3]

Philosophies of non-violence towards sentient beings are well-rooted in various strains of Buddhism and Hinduism.

But the term "vegan" was first coined in 1944 by members of the UK Vegetarian Society that were looking to separate themselves from vegetarians consuming dairy and eggs. In their first publication for their members, coined "The Vegan News,"[4] the founder Donald Watson wrote the following:

> The unquestionable cruelty associated with the production of dairy produce has made it clear that lacto-vegetarianism is but a half-way house between flesh-eating and a truly humane, civilised diet, and we think, therefore, that during our life on earth we should try to evolve sufficiently to make the "full journey". We can see quite plainly that our present civilisation is built on the exploitation of animals, just as past civilisations were built on the exploitation of slaves, and we believe the spiritual destiny of man is such that in time he will view with abhorrence the idea that men once fed on the products of animals' bodies.

While these sentences (and indeed the rest of the document) at the time did not address the use of animal-derived products other than food, it is very clear that the motivation for abstaining from dairy (and eggs) was rooted in ethical concerns about the exploitation of animals.

What is a vegan?

The Vegan Society, as the organization now is called, writes on its website,[5] that it was not until 1949 that an actual definition for the term vegan was established, which then explicitly includes "commodities, work, hunting, vivisection" and "all other uses involving exploitation" besides food production. Currently, the Vegan Society defines veganism as

> a philosophy and way of living which seeks to exclude – as far as possible and practicable – all forms of exploitation of, and cruelty to, animals for food, clothing or any other purpose; and by extension, promotes the development and use of animal-free alternatives for the benefit of humans, animals and the environment. In dietary terms it denotes the practice of dispensing with all products derived wholly or partly from animals.

Therefore, at its core, veganism is a philosophy that does not support the exploitation of animals. It is as simple as saying "I believe we should treat animals with respect the same way we try to treat other humans with respect." But the devil is in the detail. While most people might agree with the general stance that we all should treat animals nicely, the vegan philosophy, according to the definition, actively "seeks to exclude" exploitation. Basically, that means not just passively sitting around and saying "I believe in equal pay" while quietly accepting a higher paycheck than another colleague. It is seeking. It is active. Actions need to follow. It means walking up to your boss, demanding equality, and in the worst case accept a cut on our own salary for the matter of principle. In the case of veganism, these actions usually come in the form of boycott and non-participation.

The second important part of that definition is "as far as possible and practicable." When you are cornered, some say that attack is the best defense, so people will try to poke holes in your arguments during debates. Every vegan has been confronted with statements like "you also kill animals when you harvest vegetables" and similar challenges that imply that you are not being consistent or not able to uphold your own values all the time. Obviously, it is not possible to exist on this planet without leaving any traces. You will step on ants, occasionally maybe on a snail when it rains. You may even decide to have the audacity of not asking in a restaurant whether the bread on the table contains traces of butter and gamble your vegan karma by eating it. The point of "as far as possible and practicable" is that we are aware of certain practicable limits and accept them. Don't go ask your boss for a pay cut when you are already struggling to put food on your children's plates working minimum wage. So vegans don't aim for an illusion of perfection, but try to do their best. Clearly, this should not be misunderstood as a free pass to "cheat" on your vegan lifestyle – this would be inconsistent with the underlying morals, just like you cannot cheat on other immoral practices like not killing, raping, robbing, etc. At the same time, it also should be kept in mind that as a vegan you make independent decisions about your life. The Vegan Society will not come to your house and go through your stuff. There surely is room for individual interpretation where you draw the lines on certain issues. While it might be hard to justify (and kind of pointless) to call yourself a vegan and eat fish, there is much more debate about some animal-derived products like honey. Also, you may choose to continue wearing leather products that were passed down to you in the spirit of not putting them to waste, while others feel downright uncomfortable with the idea of walking around with a dead cow's skin on them. You will not be a worse vegan for whatever personal choices you make. Just don't use the term too casually, please. I've heard people say they are vegan but like to eat meat when they go to restaurants. Your choice, but there was a term invented for that: flexitarian.

The final part of the first sentence in the definition above makes explicit the fact that animal exploitation not only happens in the food industry. Animals are also exploited for fashion (think primarily fur, leather, wool, silk and feathers), for testing the safety of products intended for humans (medicine, cosmetics, etc.) and for our entertainment (zoos, circuses, races, fights, sports). Therefore, a vegan chooses not to wear jackets with down filling, shops for cosmetics that have not been tested on animals and boycotts institutions like Sea World. That's why many vegans feel slightly uneasy about people who only follow a diet without animal-derived products and call themselves vegan. Yet, the final sentence of the Vegan Society's definition takes into account the fact that the term vegan can be used "in dietary terms".

Plant-based diets and other terms

So there you have it. Such are the "vegans" for you according to how the people who started the movement defined their motivations. If we look for a definition of veganism according to more of an outside perspective, say, Wikipedia,[6] we learn that there are more specific categorizations we can make in the vegan movement: dietary veganism, ethical veganism and environmental veganism. Of course this only describes that people cite different motivations for the same behavior. But I am not really convinced that this makes sense. Yes, as long as the result is the same, the animals profit the same, so the motivation technically does not matter. But I honestly have doubts that dietary vegans will be equally consistent and enduring as ethical vegans. How many people do you know who stuck to diets? Most people stop once the desserts come out.[7] Now I do not want to come across as gatekeeper trying to keep dietary vegans out of the club. In fact, one of the criticisms that vegans often face is that our strictness of principles turns people away and that 1000 imperfect vegans would benefit the animals more than 1 perfect vegan. I do welcome anybody with open arms to adapt "imperfect" vegan behaviors today rather than strict vegan behaviors tomorrow! But in terms of names, when we talk about a label for a behavior, we need to be clear and strict. Otherwise the label becomes pointless. Not the behavior, but the name attributed to it. Also, I wonder if you can reverse-engineer labels, just because you have the same behavioral pattern? I came across a joke on the internet, where a guy answered the question "why are you vegan" with "because I hate plants".[8] So what if you don't care about animals and honestly wanted to destroy as much of the plant kingdom as possible? Obviously, that's very constructed, pointless on many levels and funnier as a joke, but would you be a vegan as a plant hater? Could you be a feminist if you simply hated men and that was your true motivation for advancing women? You may behave similarly, but I'm not sure whether you qualify to be part of the club.

In addition to subgroups of vegans, also new terms are being coined to deal with the changing perception and reality of the vegan movement. Because "vegan" can be negatively connotated among non-vegans, some businesses started using descriptors like "plant-based" to appeal to a broader audience. A plant-based burger sounds healthy, whereas a vegan burger sounds like somebody is handing you an animal-rights pamphlet between two buns. Problem solved. Only that new terms again need to go through the proof of time in order to be fleshed out (or vegged out) precisely: Does plant-based really mean "made only of plants"? Not according to the Swiss dairy board that even advocates a plant-based diet on their website, obviously trying to get a piece of the plant-based pie by arguing that a plant-based diet is mainly based on plants but should definitely be spiced up with some mother milk for baby cows and even the occasional piece of animal flesh.[9]

Also the old-school "ethical vegans" have not been sleeping on innovation. Especially social media posts now often contain the addition "FTA" after "vegan" to express that one is "vegan for the animals" as opposed to for health or environmental reasons, etc. Of course, if we go back to the definition of how the Vegan Society defined veganism, "vegan FTA" is a tautology, like a striped zebra.

Whatever your motives are, the term vegan has come a long way. Only a decade ago, it was not unusual to ask about vegan options in a restaurant and receive in return nothing but looks of confusion. Now the term is quite established, even if we seemingly cannot always agree exactly on what it really means to be a vegan.

Maybe not surprisingly, it is equally difficult to find out who these vegans are if we don't even always know what they are. Reported numbers by surveys can vary quite significantly, but it seems safe to say that in most developed nations vegans make up a percentage in the very low single digits, thus being still a small subgroup of vegetarians that can reach low double digits in some countries.[10] Also, reliable demographic reports are not easy to come by, but the somewhat stereotypical image that some reports paint of the average vegan being a young, educated woman seems plausible. It has indeed been established again and again that women sympathize more with animals, that women seem to have an easier time with their peers switching to a vegetarian or vegan diet and that women care more about healthy food choices, whereas men face more peer pressure to conform to socially established behaviors considered to be masculine.[11] In other words, men have a much harder time fighting against the well-established cultural links that tie meat consumption to masculinity. Real men eat meat, eating meat makes you strong, and salads are for women who want to watch their figure. These are the images that we have been exposed to so many times that most of us take them for granted. We unconsciously play along and contribute ourselves to uphold these learned behaviors. Adolescents in their push and pull for carving out their own identity might on the other hand still be more open to alternative life forms and education should at least in theory lead to more critical and open-minded fellow humans, who are equipped with the necessary tools to make life on this planet better for everyone.

As such a small minority with quite contrasting beliefs to those of the majority, vegans are especially one thing: others. "Otherizing" is a term that is used when we treat or view people as distinctly different from us and language plays a big role in that. It creates more distance between two groups and vegans experience it constantly. For example, people constantly make references to things that we consume versus things that they consume, certainly without bad intentions. But if somebody calls a vegan option "your food", it suggests that what we eat is different from what they eat. As if vegan food was something weird or particular and could not be eaten by non-vegans. And this goes hand in hand with what is maybe the most annoying expression we deal with all the time: "normal". It's not just "your food" vs. "my food," it is most of the time "your food" versus "normal food," contrasting what we eat with what normal people usually eat. As if there was something abnormal about a plate of spaghetti with tomato sauce. As if no meat-eater has ever eaten a salad before. There is clearly nothing "abnormal" about vegan food or a pair of non-leather shoes, yet whenever people want to make some kind of comparative statement, they tend to label the non-vegan alternative as "normal". Although this may seem like a small thing, language is obviously very powerful at creating subtle realities. Otherwise the meat, dairy and egg industry would not hide behind euphemisms like calling farm animals "livestock" as if they were a simple commodity and their slaughter "harvesting" as if they were fruit. In the English language it is still common to refer back to an animal with the pronoun "it", taking away some of its livelihood and turning animals into "something" rather than "someone". This is simply yet another layer of otherizing, only this time between animals and humans, to create more distance between the two. If language implies that vegans are "not normal" and that animals are objects rather than sentient beings, it is much easier for us to disregard the suffering of animals and dismiss the validity of the arguments that vegans make.

The common denominator for vegans and vegetarians

Before we are going to spend some time talking about the reasons for being vegan instead of vegetarian, so basically the differences between the two, I think we should first establish the commonalities and touch on some simple underlying thoughts about why both groups choose not to eat meat. The fact that we eat a cow but not a dog in most countries is purely cultural and from this, we derive legality. Morality, on the other hand, is different from legality because when we try to answer if it's right to eat an animal, we have to bring in more sound arguments than "we have been doing it forever" or "it is not illegal." Vegans and vegetarians alike argue that it is sentience, the biologically recognized fact that most species have awareness, feel pain and can suffer, that makes it wrong to willfully hurt them. In fact, many countries do have laws that protect animals from being hurt unnecessarily. It's just that all these laws know exceptions and are quite relaxed in their definitions of what is considered (un-)necessary as soon as food production is involved. Now if we were required to eat meat to survive, that would make sense – you don't want to hurt a cow, but you also don't want to die yourself, so you kill for survival and not for pleasure. But the thing is we don't. We are not carnivores but omnivores. We can eat meat but don't have to. This is really not up for debate (at least outside of the social media comment sections) – there is a large scientific consensus that in a modern world of food abundance we no longer need to hunt in order to survive. So if it's not a vital necessity, the argument eventually boils down to taste. Is it ok to kill and eat an animal because you "like" eating steak, not because you "have to"? This is where both vegans and vegetarians come up with a hard no. Five minutes of sensory pleasure while chewing on some chicken nuggets is not a morally sound justification for ending the life of a sentient being that strives to live and avoid harm. Not even to mention that this death usually follows a life of confinement, mutilation and suffering, which in itself is a crime (morally, not always legally) towards sentient beings.

Oh and one final point. Fish are not vegetables! For reasons more likely stemming from cultural traditions, but hardly animal welfare concerns, some people consider themselves vegetarian but eat fish. Or people ask vegetarians in disbelief "so you don't even eat fish???" We do have an expression for fish-but-no-meat-eaters and it is called pescatarian. Vegans and vegetarians do not eat fish as also fish are sentient beings. Just because they don't scream when you hurt them the way a dog would does not mean that they don't feel pain. And what we are doing with fish and the entire underwater world is actually even worse than what we do to land animals. The oceans are being fished empty and entire ecosystems are collapsing. We kill around 1 to 3 trillion fish per year! That's a lot of individual lives taken for us to chew on a fish stick for a few minutes and feel good about ourselves. "Fun" fact: this number is only an estimate because with fish we don't even bother counting, we just weigh the anonymous mass of "material" we catch. Currently around 200 million tons per year.[12,13]

What vegans are not

First of all: perfect. I cannot stress this enough. We do not think that we are perfect and we do not think that veganism is perfect. We are flawed people like all other people in this world, who also understand that nothing on this planet is always as simple as a black or white, yes or no solution. That being said, you will meet annoying vegans, aggressive vegans, kind vegans, friendly vegans, unfriendly vegans, skinny vegans, not so skinny vegans, sporty vegans, couch-potato vegans, smoothy-drinking vegans and pizza and coke eating vegans, you name it. So please do not reject all vegans because of a negative encounter you may have had with one person. Yes, there may be a fraction of vegans who will possibly even result to violence to defend their beliefs. Every protest movement will inevitably include people that are willing to go to different lengths to reach their goals. But I can guarantee you that the majority of vegans do not have a "by any means necessary"-mentality and reject violence against other humans just as strictly as we reject violence against animals. There may also be a fraction of vegans who may feel quirky or pseudo-religious to you because you perceive an air of spirituality around them, what some may also refer to as tree huggers. But also the weird guy in hemp sandals who doesn't shower and still uses a landline phone is not representative of all vegans. There is also a noticeable fraction of vegans who seem extremely health-conscious and promote a self-image of gym-trimmed bodies, daily yoga sessions, and seem to eat nothing but juices, smoothies and the latest super-foods. But again, they are no more representative of the vegan population as any other fraction of a population is representative of the whole group. These are not "vegans", they are "some" vegans. But unfortunately, outliers in any group, especially the loud, colorful and quirky ones, can quickly become representative of the entire movement in the public perception. And, more often than not, media representation will do the rest to put you in a certain box. I even know people who choose not to identify as vegans because they do not want to be associated with some of these stereotypes, although I personally find this a pity, given that we do not make these choices for or because of those people, but for the animals, the planet and in extension ourselves.

The stereotypes are many and typical for otherized groups mostly negative. Besides the common belief that all vegans are malnourished, pale and weak, probably the most popular stereotype we are confronted with is that we see ourselves as superior to others and are preachy. So let's dive into that!

2 Preachy vegans

Despite the inherent seriousness of the topic, I think that most vegans actually enjoy a good laugh – even at their own expense. At least the ones who have not yet lost all their muscle strength due to protein deficiency and are still physically capable of smiling. Just make it a good joke please. Trust me, you're not the first one telling us that we eat away the food of your food. These "jokes" will at best evoke a polite smile and even the palest vegan zombie will suddenly find enough strength to cancel that superficial friendship link you had on Instagram. It still may be far from the best vegan joke of all times, but it certainly is understandable why the punchline of "How do you recognize vegans? They will tell you about it!" may raise a few chuckles. It's funny because it's true. Right? The stereotype of the preachy vegan that cannot wait to let everybody in on their apparently not-so-secret secret is very persistent and if you have met a vegan in your life, chances are that it didn't take very long for you to find out about it. So are vegans inherently preachy? An arrogant bunch of know-it-alls, who like to be in the center of attention? Of course not. We've already established that vegans come from all walks of life with all kinds of personality traits and I guarantee you that the classic introvert will go to great lengths to avoid being in the center of attention, which usually means hiding the fact that one is different from the others in any way as much as possible. And that's not an easy thing to pull off, especially if you like to enjoy a meal in the company of other people. Any type of awkward inquiry about a menu item in a restaurant will give you away immediately. People seem to have some kind of superpower when it comes to spotting irregular behavior. What's the last time you had dinner with a newly pregnant person and were not immediately on to something after the food order? You don't drink alcohol today? Very odd. No raw ingredients? Busted! So good luck trying to order a pizza without cheese and getting away with it! Are you lactose intolerant? Oh, you don't like cheese? Are you a VEGAN? If you would have reacted to either one of the first two questions, chances are that the conversation you just unintentionally interrupted would continue and nobody would be too concerned about your inability to digest milk properly. But unfortunately for you, the entire restaurant just got dead silent and one of your friends' eyelids started twitching. Ok, I'm exaggerating, but I can promise you that, more often than not, it is not the vegan in the group that starts jumping up and down shouting "Everybody look at me, I'm a vegan and would like to have your opinion about it!"

Being vegan in a non-vegan world

Even more than two decades into the twenty-first century, identifying as a vegan makes you part of a very small minority. Yes, it is a growing movement and yes, more and more people are familiar with the concept, but most likely you will be the only vegan in most social gatherings – unless you actively socialize with other vegans, found a vegan significant other, etc., etc. And not only are you on your own, but your ethics also clash head on with the normal daily behavior of everybody around you. That is a lot of potential for conflict or at least strong disagreement. So most of the time I prefer not even getting into arguments. I hardly ever found that much good came from a rushed attempt at explaining my ethics in situations that are not designed to discuss serious matters. A topic as gory as the killing and exploitation of animals and as philosophical as ethics is not per se something you want to dive into on a fun night out. But, whether you want to or not, on many occasions you are at some point identified as "the vegan" and, more often than not, immediately confronted with some type of judgment, joke, comment or question. And all you really have are two options. If you want to be true to yourself, you jump on the conversation but feed into the stereotype of the preachy vegan. You are obviously going to have to state your motives, explain why in your opinion it is bad to eat meat, etc. and that is usually perceived as preachiness. Or you just let it go, smile it off, and feel bad afterwards because you did not stand up for what you believe in.

We will come to the problem that follow if you actually choose to discuss the topic more in-depth in just a bit, but for the moment let's dwell on why vegans can be "triggered" so frequently in the first place. You would be surprised how many times a day we are presented with an opportunity to bite our tongue. Well, maybe it's not all that surprising really. Humans tend to consume animals and their byproducts multiple times per day while spending hours looking at cute cat videos on the internet. And nothing triggers us vegans more than hypocrites.

Please read this without taking offense – I myself have behaved exactly like the people I'm now arrogantly labeling hypocrites here. But for the lack of a better word and because that is exactly what all of us vegans secretly think about you, let's call a spade a spade. If you are chewing on a ham sandwich and at the same time tell me how amazing your dog is, then you are exactly that: A hypocrite. There, I said it. But it's not even your fault. We all grow up in a world where we put animals into categories according to our cultural needs and liking. In most western societies, dogs belong to the lucky group that is destined for sleeping in our beds, barbershop treatments and complicated life-extending surgeries. If you were born a cow or a pig, you are less lucky. You're destined to spend your significantly shortened life ankle deep in your own filth and end up on the wrong end of that aforementioned sandwich. How absolutely ridiculous and random that distinction is can be exposed both culturally and biologically. Cats and dogs are perfectly acceptable meat sources in many parts of the world, while cows are holy untouchable deities in other parts. Yet, in the western world, we love to point our fingers at the appalling practices of those who we understand to be dog-eaters. How could you!? Well, the same could be asked about that pig you're eating because, biologically speaking, pigs and dogs are pretty much the same things. There is ample evidence that pigs are just as smart, social, trainable and emotional as dogs.[14] From firsthand experience, I can also confirm that pigs definitely enjoy a nice belly rub, just like our furry friends at home. So what is up with that? On what basis can we pretend a pig to be less worthy of life in any way than a dog? It definitely cannot be a matter of character because I constantly experience the same hypocrisy with cats. And don't get me wrong, I have nothing against cats. But cats have effectively subdued humans into their personal slaves. If you don't do EXACTLY as they command you, they will knock your precious collection of porcelain figures from the shelves, use your curtains for climbing practice and scratch your eyes out. And somehow we are perfectly fine with all this abuse, reward them with food (only the best of course) and build funny ladders from our balconies so that they can bring us dead mice as presents. I'm kidding of course. But the amount of times that people will tell you how appalled they are about certain mistreatments of dogs and cats, while apparently not even realizing their own contribution as they chew on their food in between sentences is staggering! Only recently I found myself in exactly one of these conversations where one person in the round was quite upset when somebody mentioned a cat that is being kept indoors 24/7. Fair enough, I'm perfectly willing to discuss what settings and surroundings are ideal for a specific animal's needs. But then let's be extra upset about the fact that the pig that ended up in your lunch was not only kept in a setting that is ~~probably~~ definitely not where a pig would choose to live and stay if it could but was also killed after only a few months of living. Poor indoor-cat eating lobster on a silver platter all day. On the inside, I sometimes just want to scream.

But it does not end with dogs and cats. The same happens with any animal as long as there is an easy victim to blame that is not us. That trophy hunter you saw on Facebook who went to Africa to shoot an elephant? Hang the bastard! People get very emotional and super pro-animals when they feel sorry for an individual creature that seems worthy of protection. But in the end, it's all the same. Animals die unnecessarily for human pleasure, whether it is a pleasure of taste or a pleasure of questionable wall decoration. In either case, the animal had no interest in dying. Oh, and yeah, that poor elephant, lion, polar bear or whatever you saw in the media, as sad as their stories are, they are barely worth a footnote in the headcount of how many individuals we commercially kill for food on a daily basis. If numbers are your thing, here you go: In 2019 we killed over 300'000'000 cows, over 72'000'000'000 chickens and over 1'300'000'000 pigs worldwide. Want more? Add another 3.3 billion ducks, 500 million goats, 600 million of each sheep, turkeys and rabbits, and 700 million geese.[15] And these are just the most common animals, still leaving out many smaller animal groups and not even diving into the ocean (pun intended), where we kill even more animals than on land, the roughly 2 trillion fish I mentioned earlier (that spells out 2'000'000'000'000!), again not even counting all the other marine life. I know that it's hard to imagine such amounts as individuals with a story – the individual gets lost in the group. But in the case of cows, that's 300'000'000 times the sad individual elephant that was innocently minding its own business when its life was taken. 300'000'000 times of suffering. 300'000'000 times the same emotions that your dog or cat are capable of. But most people prefer to post pictures of their dogs on social media to share with the world how much joy their companion brings into their life. Followed by another post with some kind of fake Buddhist quote on how we should all protect the planet and love each other. Followed by a photo of a nice dinner with wine and a big piece of a dead animal on their plate.

"Hypocrites!" That's all vegans think most of the day. But of course we can't tell you that because then we would be left without any friends.

And just when you thought being confronted with friends and co-workers who don't understand you was making you miserable, you open up the newspaper (or click on a news app, for all the young readers out there) and find nothing but useless anti-vegan rhetoric. Ok, not exclusively and I do have to admit that things have gotten already much better over the past decade, but the amount of negative portrayal we have to face really does not help our movement and cause at all. If a malnourished baby gets sick and the parents happened to be vegan weirdos, that makes a perfect headline in which vegans kill babies with their extreme choices. Recently, I came across an entire opinion piece in a national newspaper where the author complained that the awareness month "Veganuary" is ruining the language. So yeah, we not only kill babies, apparently we also ruin the way people speak. And these are only the more overtly negative media coverages. I am still waiting for a vegan to be interviewed in a TV show where they will not try to discredit veganism by casting doubt on its feasibility. They always find an "expert" nutritionist "Dr. so and so", who thinks it's dangerous to eat vegan, when in fact the world's biggest association for nutrition clearly states that a well-planned vegan diet is suitable for all stages of life.[16] Of course spreading doubt is a very powerful but vicious tool. For people without access to unbiased information this is nothing but validation for already existing doubt or insecurity. All it really takes is one counter-opinion to call something "controversial" or "disputed". You can have an overwhelming majority of scientists agree that global warming is a real thing but find one news anker who is willing to call it "controversial" and potentially thousands of viewers will walk away from the TV thinking that experts are not really sure about this, so therefore, they shouldn't be worried about it either. And that's what makes it so much harder for us to be understood. Page after page of paid newspaper and magazine space where the dairy industry tries to portray milk consumption as essential for human health or cow farming as a sustainable solution to environmental issues. Headline after headline where vegans are portrayed as extreme. Ad after ad where happy animals are grazing all by themselves on pastures, feeding consumers obvious lies about the reality of food production. Talk show after talk show where animal rights activists are belittled, animal farmers deny any involvement in well-documented animal cruelty and the bottom line somehow always seems to be that all the present people eat only locally sourced food produced in the best country in the world and therefore we should all keep calm and carry on. That's what we are up against. But I am still convinced that the truth will prevail and that we have gathered enough momentum to reach more and more people. The science is out there, the images and videos of abusive practices are out there and the knowledge is out there. All it takes is for people not to look away any longer and face the reality. My recommendation? An extremely graphic but very powerful documentary called *Earthlings*,[17] narrated by Oscar winner Joaquin Phoenix. Looking directly into the eyes of an animal that is about to be killed is one of the most sobering experiences you can have in a world where food production is so far detached from our daily reality. It is the only documentary I ever watched that literally brought tears to my eyes and it was the last nail in the coffin on my switch to veganism.

Early "enthusiasm"

So yeah, it can be a pretty lonely endeavor to go vegan and most of the time you may choose not to step on anybody's toes for the sake of peace. But so where does the stereotype of the preachy vegan come from if we all shut up most of the time as I claim? I would argue that there are probably two factors at play. First of all – perception is not only dependent on the sender and I do believe that the receiver plays an important role in this case especially. Every vegan has experienced this situation: you are talking with a meat-eater or many meat-eaters and your cover gets blown, your attempts at hiding your true identity fail, you are compromised. Either you've been pointed out by a third party or some turn of events made you insert the comment that you are a vegan. And then, without any further comments or questions from your side, the meat-eater will say something along the lines of "oh I also only eat very little meat" or "oh I only buy my meat from the local farmer." Of course there is nothing wrong with that statement except for the fact that it is most of the time complete self-delusion and that it reveals how people truly feel about your sheer presence: They feel guilty. Your presence makes them uncomfortable about their own actions. "I only eat very little meat" is code for "I too am a good person". They feel judged without you saying a word. Does that make the vegan preachy or is it the non-vegan person that feels attacked before you even say a word? Not for me to decide, but just some food for thought.

Then there are preachy vegans. Of course there are! And I would argue that most vegans are preachy at a certain stage of their journey, namely at the very beginning. Imagine you live a normal happy life and one day you have a realization. Maybe you saw a documentary, read a book, talked with a friend, whatever. You suddenly realize that pigs are like your beloved dog or that chickens are not too dissimilar from your cat. You understand that eating meat is a choice and not a default or necessity. You saw the suffering that is going on behind closed doors. You suddenly feel actual empathy with each and every individual that is unnecessarily killed. You now have a completely shifted view of the world. Your surroundings, the people you spend time with, that are close to you, your friends, coworkers and family, everybody is chewing happily on steaks while for you a piece of meat now represents the brutal, unnecessary and unjustified death of a sentient being. On the one hand, you understand their blindness towards their actions because you too have been doing the same thing until only recently, but on the other hand, you now just gained a lot of knowledge that you think they obviously must not be having. So you want to share. You want them to know what you know. Everything is very fresh in your head because you probably didn't stop at the documentary you watched. You went down the rabbit hole on the internet because you probably had some questions yourself. Most likely you did your fair share of research before taking such a "drastic" decision of giving up so many things you've been accustomed to consuming. That's when you may forget for a moment that other people have possibly never seriously dealt with this topic and find it pushy if you come to them trying to make them see what for you now is such an obvious thing.

Pause. Rewind. Play. At the fear of being repetitive here, I really want to stress and make you understand how vegans see the world around them because this is kind of the core that explains most of our behavior. So if you want to understand vegans, try to think about this again very carefully and put yourself in our shoes, looking at the situation from our perspective. If you take on the position that taking the life of an animal is wrong, therefore sad or tragic, then you will want to make other people stop. It's as simple as that. It's actually natural behavior. If you see somebody mistreat a dog, most people would intervene. If somebody mistreats a child, we definitely intervene. If we are exposed to injustice, mistreatment and brutality, we want it to end. I really don't want to make direct comparisons with human atrocities throughout history because I don't intend to minimize human suffering or suggest that both are one and the same thing. But I think you can get an idea of how helpless people must feel who witness tragedies unfold around them with nobody around to stop the madness. This is "similar" (not equal) to how vegans can feel about the world around them. They see a tragedy in their eyes (billions of sentient animals in captivity, mistreated and slaughtered) and feel helpless that nobody around them is willing to see. So you want to make them see. You talk, you get emotional, you want them to stop looking the other way. Not because you want to be annoying. Not because you think you are superior. But simply because you want the madness to stop.

I have certainly been there and I have experienced other new vegans go through this stage of early "enthusiasm".

It's part of your identity shaping. You have new values that will get scrutinized and need to be defended. So while the meat-eater is trying to defend their identity as somebody who is not a vegan, you are trying to defend and shape yours. Once a vegan gets more settled in their identity and has understood that they cannot change the world around them by arguing with friends, they usually become quite tame human beings. A bit like an adolescent that leaves the rebellious youth behind, gives up on that dream of becoming an artist and settles for that boring 9 to 5 office job. That's great news for the people around you, but only so-so for the animals, who really have nobody else fighting for them other than those humans who choose to do so in their name. Think about it. If humans see injustice, we have the police to help us, we can try to address issues with government bodies or NGOs, we can draw media attention to what is going on, we potentially can get people at the other end of the world to try to improve our local problem on this end. Animals have zero. They are 100% at our mercy. Pigs cannot get the cows involved to help them gang up against the farmer. They cannot reason with the guy who is about to end their life. Vegans is all they have. So without trying to make this sound like we're all that and more, all I'm saying is, next time you feel that a vegan is preachy, think about if it's really so annoying that a person is speaking up for innocent living beings. Is it not a noble act?

People respond to different inputs but I guess it's fair to say that most people tend not to react too positively if they are getting yelled at. That's why many vegans actively advocate the idea of leading by example through positivity. They end up writing food blogs, open up restaurants, or just silently live their vegan lives hoping that others will realize how stylish their non-leather shoes are and how tasty that tofu stir-fry tastes and follow suit. And that's certainly not the worst strategy. Tobias Leenaert wrote a fantastic book about how he believes that pragmatism is the most successful road to positive change and a vegan world.[18] But if there weren't any vegans who remain angry enough that they cannot swallow their feelings, there would not be much of an animal rights movement, I guess. It takes a lot of passion, conviction and anger to dedicate your life to fighting with people on a regular basis. But it's those people who contribute for example the oh-so-important undercover videos from what's going on behind closed doors on farms and slaughterhouses, who might be even willing to break the law to give people in their comfortable living rooms a glance of what it means to be an animal destined for a short, gruesome life and an early death.

So if you interact with a vegan that seems a bit preachy, please understand that they are not angry at you per se, they understand that you are living in a world where what you do is normal. But they are deeply wounded by the fact that society as a whole seems to think that a fashionable shoe is a good reason to murder an animal and remove its skin.

Probably due to the preachiness people sometimes experience and the rather strong conviction most vegans have about their choices, one often hears comparisons between veganism and religion. Some social science scholars even claimed veganism to fit the legal criteria of a religion.[19] Opponents of veganism like to link us to religion for our attempts at "converting" non-vegans. And if you ask sociologists, they will readily explain the attraction of movements like veganism due to the growing absence of religion in modern western societies, arguing that people turn to alternatives to faith in order to get a sense of belonging. Now I do not negate that vegans may feel they belong more when they are surrounded by like-minded people than not, but that's almost obvious. We all like to feel the comfort of peers who understand our feelings. But it's hard to see how this should be a motivator as most of the time you mostly end up feeling like you don't belong. And I would strongly disagree with putting veganism in a corner anywhere near religion. We do not follow any leaders or answer to any higher powers and there is no "belief" involved whatsoever. That most animals are sentient and much more similar to us than people believed in the past is a biological fact. Acknowledging that animals don't enjoy being caged, separated from their families, cut, chained, whipped or killed, means to follow science. Drawing the conclusion from this knowledge that we should therefore not hurt them is philosophical and political but definitely not spiritual. Psychologist Melanie Joy came up with an interesting framework to make more sense of contextualizing the vegan idea in the modern world. She argues that we should acknowledge that it is not only vegans who follow a set of values and make a choice to do so, but also meat-eaters. The problem, in her opinion, is a lack of a label for the majority behavior, which makes it of course easier to single out those who make the choice to go vegan as "others". She coined the term "carnism" in opposition to veganism, arguing that also meat-eaters make daily choices and that not only vegans "indoctrinate" (as we are often accused) but that also meat-eaters are actively taught the carnist belief system from early on in order to justify its patterns as normal, natural and necessary.[20] Simple example? Most people find it wrong per se to harm animals and have strong emotions against showing young kids footage of slaughterhouses. Yet, we teach our kids that it's ok to eat what results from that practice, so we obviously do make very active (even if possibly subconscious) choices and decisions to keep up our carnist worldview. And the fact that we do have a choice becomes extremely apparent the very moment a vegan steps into the room. The presence of a vegan reminds meat-eaters that other behaviors are possible and breaks up the safe status-quo environment of undisturbed carnism, which is probably a big part of the reason why some meat-eaters tend to get a bit defensive in the presence of vegans. It's a pattern that we experience in all walks of life and maybe one of the biggest reasons why diversity is such an asset. Different perspectives may open our eyes to viewpoints and ideas we would have never even considered in our limited status quo experience that we have on this planet without exposure to other cultures, beliefs, generations and lifestyles.

The difficulty of discussing veganism with non-vegans

Sooner or later (probably sooner than later) you will need to have "the talk" with your family and friends. Not THAT talk, I hope they know about the birds and the bees. Although you probably will end up talking about bees as well, but you get the point. So you need to tell people that you no longer eat meat, drink dairy, consume eggs, wear leather, or go to zoos. Probably no more honey either because also bees are your friends now. In other words, you are now what they might consider a person that is "extreme" in their choices. Of course you have your reasons and all the arguments lined up to defend and explain why you made that decision, but at the very core of that discussion, no matter how you phrase it, you imply judgment. It's common advice to formulate personal opinions as non-factual statements to make the recipient understand that you are not a know-it-all, but just voice a personal viewpoint. But as politely, personal and indirect you formulate your "in my humble opinion I consider the unnecessary slaughtering of sentient beings wrong"-statement, what it implies to the hearer is that you therefore consider them a brutal murderer deprived of morals. The problem is that once you start talking about motivation and reasons, it's more than just what's on your plate. There is not much room for personal preferences when you talk about morals. You are with us or against us – that's the core reality of the argument. Just like you will probably agree that the killing of other humans is never acceptable, also not on a weekends-only basis, or in small quantities, it is very similar when we defend the rights of animals to live. If you take on the vegan standpoint that it is not right to take an animal's life for your pleasure, then Meatless Mondays, "I only buy local", and vegetarians are all not with you, but against you. Not in the sense of enemies, of course, but in the sense of (dis-)agreement on morals. This black-and-white ethics is what makes your vegan presence so problematic for many non-vegans. You don't judge them actively, but your stance implies that you must consider them to be on the wrong end of something that only has two options, and this can be also hurtful to the non-vegan person who maybe shared many food experiences with you in the past or maybe even raised you (to the best of their knowledge and abilities) as a non-vegan.

Reality for most vegans is of course not as brutal, we don't either hate or love the people around us. Veganism is part of our identity, not our whole identity. Plus, we perfectly understand that we are in a minority with our opinion and can only reach the majority of people step by step. If you stop eating meat on Mondays, that's one day less in the grand scheme and a few less animals that will die, so yeah, all in all, that is progress. It just does not make any sense morally. But we are willing to look past that and acknowledge your will to improve the world in baby steps. You could also say that we are so desperate that we will take anything we get. You started ordering oat milk cappuccinos because they are trendy? You're a hero! Keep up the good work. But still, I would argue that many vegans feel a bit schizophrenic about their own behavior. Exactly because we understand that every ally along the way is helpful, we have to be lenient in our "judgment" of others. Exactly because we already carry the label of preachy extremists, we don't want to feed into that stereotype. So yes, no matter whether you are vegan for the environment, for health reasons, or actually for the animals, you are of course a welcome ally. But at the same time, I think many ethically motivated vegans still feel kind of righteous about their motivation and understandably so. Not because we are better people, but because we believe that veganism is not a diet but a practical philosophy that only works as such if you follow through, if you are fully accountable for what you preach. That's why we still feel a bit of an itch and need to suppress our emotions when people say things like "oh I'm also vegan most of the time" or "I'm almost vegan myself except for....". That will really get our eyelids twitching. Not because it isn't positive, but because there's no such thing as an almost vegan, just like there's no such thing as an almost non-racist. Imagine THAT conversation! "Oh, you believe in equality? Yeah me too, totally, I'm actually not a racist most of the time either! Sometimes, on the weekends, I allow myself a little bit of bigotry, but other than that, totally not a racist either." Again, we really appreciate the effort and no disrespect, but we're very protective of the label "vegan" and the behavior it should entail. And obviously, this pisses people off. They think we act holier-than-thou and consider ourselves superior to other people. But that's not even what this is about, it's just about pointing out that we do not see ourselves as followers of a diet where people will have cheat days or that this is about ourselves. It's about others, those that cannot fight for themselves because their voice is not heard. It is a core pillar of how you see the world, a core belief about what fairness and equality means. A roadmap of compassion, empathy and respect. Something that should technically not even be negotiable and therefore also not up for only partial subscription. Part of understanding vegans is understanding this inner struggle that many of us have, where we feel like the solution to so many problems would be so easy, if people only listened with an open mind. We're highly frustrated that nobody around us sees what we see and that then we need to go out into the world and preach watered-down messages in order to get at least a handful of people on board because nobody will listen if we let out our raw and unmonitored emotions.

I've been tied up in enough emotional debates to understand that "the talk" can be difficult. It's like discussing politics. If the other side is convinced of a completely opposing view and has their ideologies all lined up with their behavior, then it's a tough battle. Almost everybody will acknowledge that it is wrong to hurt animals and make them suffer, yet there seems to be a whole myriad of reasons why we should all keep calm and carry on. I am not trying to paint a picture here of a hopeless society where nobody can talk to each other anymore – I had many talks with friends that did not feel like there was any personal grudge resulting from this difference of opinion. But it is a very substantial difference of opinion, one that can alienate you from other people in the worst case! I am all in favor of talking respectfully with people from all walks of life and I find it important that people with different world views are able to sit down at a table together for a meal. The thing is that reality is often more complicated. With some friends you may only have a good time if certain topics are tiptoed around and that can also be fine to some degree. But if a friend or family member has a true interest in a relationship with you, it is your right to be understood. Not for them to change their view. They have all the right to have a different opinion of course. But they should at least be willing to understand your motivation, maybe even read up on the topic, just to show an interest in who you are. After all, how can we pretend to truly care about another person if we are not willing to listen and understand why they hold a position that is so essential, dominant and defining in their life every single day? If that interest is not shown at all, maybe then the relationship is not what you think it is. And the jokes? Well, if they are at least good, feel free to laugh. If they are not, there's nothing wrong with actually stating that they are hurtful. Because that's what they often are. Not because we don't want to be funny and serious all the time, but because they signal to us that we are not being taken serious for something that is essential to our own self. Veganism is not an ugly sweater that can be made fun of among good friends, but an essential part of someone's identity. And as such, it should be off-limits for ridicule as a baseline and only be crossed if you are very confident that the recipient will share the humor.

While it can be already hard enough to deal with all of this one-on-one, it may come hardly as a surprise that social gatherings like office parties or reunions can be stressful events for vegans. Especially "brutal" are family dinners that involve local traditions like Christmas, Easter, Thanksgiving, or anything like that, since it's the perfect mixing bowl of expectations from all sides. Maybe your parents really hope you'll not mess with the long tradition of eating a particular dish while you really would hope to be understood by the people that are closest to you. Mix in a couple of provocative comments from any side and the disaster is perfect. Many vegans do fear these moments, especially very early in their transition, because confronting people with new realities is always difficult. I think there is also no easy fix for this, except understanding that you do not HAVE to have a big discussion around this topic if it gets out of hand. You can also agree to disagree. I believe that most friends and family members will come to terms with your new reality sooner than later, once they realize that you are not only going through a phase and trying to mess with them but that this is now simply the new you.

3 I can understand vegetarian, but vegan?

By now, vegetarians are so established in most societies that they hardly raise eyebrows anymore. It's straightforward, you eat what everybody else eats, with one exception: meat. Given that even the most remote restaurant will probably have something on their menu that vegetarians can eat, nobody will ask a lot of questions either. So, unless you don't like the taste of meat or are on some kind of diet, you are simply one of these sensitive people who get all sad when animals are killed and therefore choose not to eat them. Straightforward. Even the most simple-minded person should understand that a steak is a piece of an animal that had to be killed in order to end up on your plate. They still may not agree with you, but at least the connection between your "problem" and your behavior should be clear to them. Not surprisingly, it's a whole other ballgame if you are a vegan. All vegans have heard the good old "I can understand vegetarian, but vegan!?!? Isn't that a bit extreme?"

Vegans are extreme

When people ask you "isn't that extreme?", they are not asking you a question of course. They are voicing their opinion and hide it behind a question. Not too many people will tell you straight to your face that you are an extremist. But if people understand the rationale of vegetarianism, why is it that veganism seems so extreme? Probably because the other products that vegans choose not to consume and use are less directly linked to the life of an animal in the public perception. What's wrong with an egg? No chicken needs to die to lay an egg, right? Same with milk, it comes from a living cow! If you have never dealt with the food industry in-depth, I can see how this logic seems legit. Commercials for the respective products have done a fantastic job suggesting that our food comes from idyllic tiny farms, where the only chicken that lives there will basically carry its egg to your breakfast table itself. Or that cookies are baked by an elderly lady with much love and care piece by piece. But what I am about to tell you may come as a shock to you, so you may want to sit down for this one: This is NOT how food gets into thousands of supermarkets at the costs you are willing (and maybe able) to pay. We will deal with the details of what is going on with dairy, eggs, etc. just a few lines further down, but here's a little spoiler: animals suffer and die also for the specific industry branches that do not only make use of their body as flesh. That is the whole reason why we defined veganism earlier as a philosophy, a lifestyle choice if you wish, whereas vegetarianism does not go beyond a dietary choice.

But before going over some of the most central arguments why vegetarianism is not enough from an ethical point of view, I would like to dwell on the perception of extremism for a second. Extremism is very closely related to another argument that I hear often, namely that everything should be done in moderation, which again suggests that being vegan is beyond moderate and thus unnecessarily strict, exaggerated or "extreme". Granted, the moderation argument makes sense in many walks of life. But again, I think these people are missing the point of the underlying motivation of veganism. Yes, if you think this is a dietary choice and I'm not drinking milk for health reasons, strict avoidance might be unnecessary and the occasional slice of cheese might be just fine. With ethics as a motivator, this just does not add up though. Again, we can easily demonstrate this if we applied this logic to an area where we have reached more social agreement that causing harm to others is not ok: us and our fellow humans. Nobody would say "I agree, killing others is wrong, but please, everything in moderation. The occasional murder has never hurt nobody". If you agree that it is wrong in principle, it does not allow for exceptions. So what we are talking about is not the overeager pursuit of preferences, but simply being consistent in one's own beliefs.

In fact, it would be very easy to make the opposite accusation of vegans being extreme towards non-vegans. Is it not a bit extreme to artificially bring sentient animals into this world with the sole purpose of killing them again shortly thereafter? Billions and billions of times per year?

To mutilate them, to make them suffer, to abuse them, without real necessity? We're not living in caves anymore and benefit from shooting the occasional buffalo. We are past the point of nutritional necessity, we don't need animal skins to keep warm, we are talking about the pure pleasure of taste and preference for materials for which we accept the suffering and death of an animal that WE put on this earth in the first place. Seems pretty extreme to me. But that's just me. Apparently, the majority of people find it more extreme to abstain from hurting animals and eating vegetables instead or, God forbid, a plant-based burger.

Reasons for being vegan

Let's talk facts. What I am about to describe here are standard commercial practices around the world, with of course some variations in terms of what is legally possible. Just to give you an example, whereas in the European Union you are allowed to farm between 33kg and 42kg of chickens per square meter indoors (depending on additional criteria on infrastructure), the US does not even have a legal limit but only recommendations of similar proportions (depending on the stage of growth of the chicken, meaning that older and bigger birds simply get less space).[21,22] That's about the size of a standard piece of paper as living space for one animal. So usually, the differences are only a matter of where the system is more screwed up – even if every local politician will assure you that the laws in their respective countries are particularly strict and much better than everywhere else, so consumers should really not worry too much and just buy "local".

You will absolutely be able to find exceptions to what I'm sketching here as a simple overview and you will find much more extensive material about your respective country from your local animal rights organizations. But again, the point here is not to describe how your weird cousin is raising two chickens in her backyard and only eats one of their eggs when the moon is full, but how millions and millions of eggs end up on the shelves of your supermarket of choice. No matter how local you might tell yourself you are eating, if you shop at a supermarket, there is no way you are eating eggs that came from your cousin's happy chickens.

Dairy

Milk first. Or let's say dairy because this milk is of course afterwards transformed into many other products such as yogurts, cheese, butter, you name it. The first point that is important to understand is that cows don't just produce milk because they are cows. I know this might sound silly, but the image of the milk-giving cow with its full udders is culturally so ingrained in many people's minds that surprisingly many adults are not even aware of the fact that cows, like any other mammal (humans included), produce milk under one sole condition and for one sole purpose only: after pregnancy, in order to feed a baby. No, cows will not explode if you don't milk them, even if it may seem that way looking at the udders of a poor modern super-cow that has been bred to produce way more milk than natural. But if we want to milk a cow, we first need to get her pregnant. And since we live in a world where time is money, nobody wants to wait until a bull has impregnated hundreds of cows to run a semi-productive milk farm. So one poor person on the farm (I guess they draw straws to determine the lucky loser) with the bull sperm in their hands needs to get the job done. I spare you here the visual description of the procedure and why the glove goes all the way to the elbow. The unwillingly impregnated cow will eventually give birth to a baby cow. What a happy occasion! Unfortunately, she won't get to spend much time with her baby, because baby cows have the annoying habit of wanting to drink their mother's milk and that's quite inconvenient. After all, we impregnated the cow so that WE could drink her milk. What to do, what to do… Well, for starters, the baby cow needs to disappear, we do not want the mother to get too attached to her baby, right? The fact that mother cows sometimes moo for days after this separation probably has nothing to do with them desperately calling for their offspring, probably they are just thanking the farmer for the wonder of birth. The newborn has one of two destinies. If it's female, it has good chances of following her mother's footsteps and one day becoming a "milk cow" herself. If it's male, it will end up on your plate as veal. Also the mother cow will end up slaughtered as soon as her efficiency as milk machine decreases, which is of course years before her natural life expectancy, but not before she likely suffered from udder infections and the likes. And that's why you cannot buy milk products without the same blood on your hands as a meat-eater. The milk industry IS the meat industry. In fact, it is arguably worse than the meat industry because it abuses the "milk cows" much longer than animals directly destined for meat production.

Eggs

Eggs are up next. Where is the harm in an egg, you may ask? Chickens lay eggs anyway, so we take a few and no harm is done. Right? Wrong. Again, this may hypothetically work if you have a chicken in your backyard and eat one egg every first Monday of the month or so. But in order to fill up these egg cartons that need to go to the supermarket shelves, we need many more eggs than you and the chicken can handle. Here's how it works in a nutshell. You cram many many chickens together in as little space as possible (space is money, just like time), of course only after you bred them for "optimized" productivity (an industrial super chicken will lay about 300 eggs per year, compared to indigenous hens at around 50 and their wild ancestors who laid even fewer eggs)[23] and possibly debeak them, so they don't go berserk on each other. Apart from the outside stress of living in such confinement, also the mass production of eggs takes quite the toll on their bodies, as a lot of energy (and calcium) goes into the production of the egg. As a female reader you probably sympathize with the physical toll of a process not dissimilar that also humans go through. If you are a man and have problems imagining that something as natural as the production of an egg causes agony and stress, just ask a woman close to you how she feels about once a month for a few days. While you're at it, you could also suggest increasing the frequency of that cycle a bit, to say 300 times a year, and see how much enthusiasm will come your way. Anyway, these tortured super-chickens will lay egg after egg for around a year and as soon as their bodies can no longer keep up with this high demand and the resulting eggs become too fragile for commercial transportation, the farmer has to do the same thing that you would do with a computer that no longer performs as desired. It's time for a replacement. "Replacement" is a euphemism I use here to avoid too much repetition of the word killing, which seems to come up a lot when you talk about food production involving animals. But it gets worse! We haven't even thought about where these egg-laying hens are coming from. After all, just like milk cows, they are again all female chickens. I could now elegantly lead over to a brief excursion about an apparent weird perversion that female animals are exploited for their reproductive "outputs", whereas not many people to my knowledge seem to have too much interest in consuming corresponding male "outputs". But I leave that up to your fantasy. Anyway, please excuse my detour. Despite the seeming sexism in animal agriculture, it is actually the male offspring that are arguably the real losers here. "Arguably" because at least they are spared a life full of abuse. What happens in the production of hens for egg farming is that as soon as the baby chickens hatch, they are sorted by gender and all the males get eliminated. Eliminated as in gassed and discarded or, even worse, SHREDDED ALIVE! This is not a made-up horror story. In many commercial chicken productions around the world,

I can understand vegetarian, but vegan?

small, yellow, fluffy, innocent baby chickens end up on conveyor belts that carry them directly into gigantic grinders. Why? Because males don't lay eggs and are useless. The meat industry won't touch them either, because these chickens are "optimized" (bred) for maximized egg production, not for maximized gain on body size a.k.a. muscle meat. It's hard to imagine an economically more worthless existence if not even a fast-food chain known for chicken wings will say "oh ok, give me at least the wings, we need millions of those." It's too expensive to raise a skinny male chicken for the meat industry and nobody wants millions of pet roosters either. Sucks for the male half of the almost 8 billion chickens that are produced for the egg industry every year.[24] But yeah, how about that egg benedict though, it's so delish! Just to wrap this up and recap, for every egg-laying hen, there was one non-egg-laying brother that had to die. And if you think this does not happen where you live, go to your closest egg farm and ask where all the male chickens ended up. It won't take Sherlock Holmes to solve that murder mystery of the missing individuals. Luckily, at least the shredding of living chickens gets banned in more and more places and the industry seems to make advancements with identifying the sex pre-birth. Also hybrid chickens for both egg and meat production seem to have a bit of momentum going for them in some very small niche markets. But this tiny step in the right direction is mainly one thing – an admittance that what we are currently doing is maybe "not quite ok".

Honey

This leaves us at honey before moving on to the non-food aisle of the supermarket and this is where it gets a bit tricky. Not because it isn't obvious that honey is a product made by animals and therefore almost by default not vegan, but because here we need to dive into the whole discourse of categorization of animals. As a vegan you get to hear excuses that range from the idea that "all animals" are not equal to humans and therefore can be eaten to the opposite extreme that "plants feel pain too," suggesting that all living creatures suffer equally, again justifying the eating of animals by saying that vegans cause as much suffering by eating "grass". Vegans obviously draw the line somewhere in between because we claim that it is not ok to kill a cow while we are ok with "killing" other living organisms such as plants, bacteria, etc. So where to draw the line and why? Well, first of all, biology, second of all, the definition of veganism. You do not need a Ph.D. in biology to understand some of the fundamental features that we share with many animals, especially those animals that very obviously resemble us in the way their bodies are constructed: A brain, a central nervous system, and some legs that will let you escape a dangerous situation. Of course, I'm simplifying here, but I do not plan to venture into a deep conversation about biology here and bore you with nervous systems, etc. However, everybody who has seen a dog or a cat getting hurt knows perfectly well that they are like humans in the sense that they register the pain, are very unhappy about it and therefore try to avoid it, probably squeaking in agony along the process. They will run away if you let them or counterattack you to make you stop. Next time you raise a hand against your house plant, you may notice something strange. It does not run away. No squeaking, no signs of agony. It is obviously an entirely different type of living organism. Yes, it is alive. But without a brain, without a nervous system, it can be quite safely assumed that they do not suffer equally as a monkey or a mouse. So vertebrates are all behaving similarly enough to us and are physically built similarly enough to our body blueprint that even kids understand their capacity to suffer. Or as experts would call it, they are "sentient beings", meaning that they have the capacity to have feelings. Other living organisms like bacteria work very very differently. And then there is a bit of middle ground or actually a lot of middle ground, as they make up the majority of the animal kingdom: Invertebrates. That includes all the insects, crustaceans such as shrimps and lobster, squids, worms, and many more. While their nervous systems differ greatly at individual levels and the jury is still out on many species regarding their subjective experience of pain, there is also strong evidence for many members of this group that does prove their capacity to suffer. Hence some recent tiny advances in the protection of lobsters from being boiled alive in restaurants.[25] So what about bees? It might well be the case that they cannot suffer pain in the exact same sense we humans do. That probably leaves us with a bit of ethical middle ground decision-making room regarding whether we find it acceptable to steal honey from bees that they produced for personal food storage, a process that will inevitably also result in some casualties among the hive. Human "farmed" beehives are prone to diseases and the handling of so many small insects will always leave some individuals hurt or squashed. Personally, besides the fact that vegans generally choose not to support commercialized breeding of animals and any form of exploitation, I like to "err on the side of caution" in terms of sentience and prefer not to infringe too much on the life of these amazing creatures. Why amazing? While most animals do have some capability of communication, one aspect that they usually lack and only humans possess is displacement – the capability to talk about something that does not happen in the here and now. Bees can. They can communicate the existence of a food source to their peers in terms of direction and distance to help them find the way. Pretty cool, no? Also, bees as pollinators are of course indispensable for our entire ecosystem. But not necessarily the honeybee! While there are thousands of bee species in the wild, the western honeybee should be viewed more like livestock rather than wildlife. They are a highly bred commercialized species that in fact can cause more harm to the ecosystem than good. They are direct competition to the wild local pollinators and spread diseases. Thus, all the local honey producers may really be doing a disservice to the environment.[26] Anyway, if you do choose to eat honey, you probably will pass the vegan test in some people's minds, in others' not. Again, veganism is about avoiding suffering and minimizing harm to animals and doing so as far as possible and practicable. That probably means you should be nice to bees and not steal their honey, after all, we are again talking about a non-necessity. But it definitely does not mean that you need to let dangerous bacteria take over your body. And it even less so means that you cannot eat broccoli "because it feels pain".

Fur

Let's move on to non-food items. I'm going to start easy on you with something that you may already agree to be bad, even if you are not vegan: fur. I think the reason that fur is a bit more stigmatized is probably because it is an easy target or at least was. Fur coats especially are very much an upper-class item associated with snobbish rich people and probably too expensive for many consumers to buy in the first place. Nothing is easier than disliking something that you do not, cannot or will not have yourself anyway, right? So if we hear somewhere that fur is bad or cruel and we think of grumpy old ladies in their fur coats instead of ourselves, it is easy to get on board and just go with the flow and agree. I do not want to downplay the fact that fur is indeed not the most ethical product, but rather look for a possible explanation why fur somehow seems to be easier to ditch than let's say leather – but we will deal with the latter in just a bit. Why is fur bad? Well, quite obviously because somebody is literally raising and killing animals for the sole purpose of skinning them. Big farms with minks, foxes, chinchillas, and other cute furry creatures crammed into cages do nothing else than breeding these innocent animals and then killing them again to use their fur for clothes. That seems quite unnecessary given that we have other things to make clothes from. The problem, unfortunately, is not limited to the old grumpy ladies in their mink coats or a handful of rappers in music videos but augmented by the gigantic demand for smaller accessories. Like the linings of winter coat hoods that many people believe to be fake, but often sadly are not. Luckily, more and more fashion brands took a stance over the last few years and started ditching fur in their collections.

Leather

But... if many people seem to feel at least somewhat bad about wearing fur and get the idea that it's maybe not the nicest thing to skin animals to turn them into fashion, how come pretty much every single non-vegan person is walking around with animal skins on their feet, uses animal skins to tighten their pants, stores coins in folded animal skin, or carries around animal skins with handles? Beats me. Well, I have some theories, of course, namely the aforementioned bias that makes us more likely to criticize something that we are not using ourselves. Maybe leather also just has not been talked about enough by animal rights groups. But it's quite literally the same thing as fur, just minus the hair. You may argue now that leather is a byproduct of the meat industry and therefore just a clever and sustainable way of avoiding waste. Unfortunately, that is often the case. But even if we assume that the leather and the meat industry were great cooperators, how do you distinguish one from the other? If we establish the baseline premise of veganism that we should not kill animals needlessly, what difference does it make who put in the order of "one fresh dead cow, please," the butcher or the shoemaker? All we end up doing is labeling one of them as the bad guy and giving the other one a free pass with the excuse that they just use the leftovers. If you happened to witness a bank robbery and pick up some of the loose money the robbers drop on the street, you are still stealing, even if the bank "already lost the money anyway because of the robbers." So should you get on board with the idea that eating meat is problematic, then it really does not make a lot of sense to keep walking around in leather shoes. Another fun fact: leather is relatively untransparent as an industry. On most items you do not find any information about what type of leather you are buying and apparently, once processed, it's hard to distinguish different skins. Or did you know that you buy kangaroo skin when you opt for some soccer shoe models by one of the biggest brands out there?[27] They "just do it" and now you know. Especially dog lovers might be upset to learn that leather of Chinese origin, where most leather comes from, can potentially even stem from dogs.[28] Still not convinced? Well, leather is not only bad for the animals that lose their skin (and their lives), but it's also terrible for both the environment and the people who work in the producing industry. If you thought leather was this great natural product and leather imitations are evil plastic, then think again. Animal skins need quite a bit of human intervention to become long-lasting jackets. And the chemicals used during that process are quite toxic, pollute the rivers and water systems nearby the factories and produce fumes that are quite detrimental to the health of the workforce, to put it mildly.[29] Unfortunately, it's everywhere, from couches to car seats. But the good news is that also here a lot of progress has been made. Synthetic materials are getting better and better. Keep in mind that also here the general truth applies that you get what you pay for. So ideally you don't shop for cheap, fast fashion that won't last more than a season (whether you are vegan or not). And instead of leather imitations made from plastic, you can now buy plant-based leather substitutes with great biodegradability, for example made from apple peel!

Wool & silk

Let's stay in the fashion industry and talk about two types of garments that give vegans an itch: wool and silk. Both are obviously of animal origin. With silk, it's quite a simple story. The standard practice of harvesting the silk from the producing silkworms is to boil them once they have cocooned up for transforming into a moth. So the only way you can talk your way into making this semi-acceptable is if you try to argue along the line of insects being less developed than vertebrates, as we talked about with honey.[30] But you'd still be saying that insects are basically not worthy of life and we can do with them whatever we want. Your call. With wool, it's a somewhat more complicated story. Similar to the "milk cow," it is today's common perception that sheep simply produce wool and we, therefore, need to liberate them of their coats and might as well use this material. But, you guessed correctly, there's a but. It would be quite strange if

I can understand vegetarian, but vegan?

evolution brought about an animal that without human intervention would just grow a gigantic amount of hair and eventually would disappear under its own mountain of fur, no? Of course the hair that does not naturally shed is a result of human breeding, so it's not an amazing natural resource as wool advocates like to sell it, but a resource we created. I agree that shaving an animal is not too intrusive, if done carefully, gently and at the right time of the year – a winter shave can be lethal in cold areas. So if your local farmer happened to own a couple of sheep and makes some mittens with the wool that now needs to be removed, that's probably not a huge problem ethically speaking. But, this is where I need to reiterate the important point that we are not talking about what technically is possible on a small scale, but what is actually, truly happening on a global commercial scale. Because that merino wool turtleneck you bought at the mall last week was definitely not made from your neighbor's wool. Big production volumes inevitably lead to pressure on the production process. Everything needs to be faster and cheaper. Good luck trying to shave hundreds of sheep with time pressure one after the other. Every person who shaved under time pressure knows exactly how this is going to end: cuts, blood and band-aids. But the rough handling of sheep is not even the worst practice. Humans maximize everything for profit, so we apparently also thought it would be a good idea to increase the skin surface per sheep in order to "harvest" more product per animal. These skinfolds are especially problematic around the anus, where parasitic infestations of fly larvae tend to occur, so we simply cut the extra skin off, a practice called mulesing. Google it! So the next time you stand in a fashion store and you see all these wool items laid out in front of you, not only from sheep but also goats (cashmere), alpacas, or simply "special" sheep (merino), think about the fact that this wool was not simply gently petted off the back of a solitary sheep, but more likely taken from a suffering animal.

Feathers

A simple variation of the fur, skin and hair we remove from animals for our own benefit are feathers. From winter coats to pillows, feathers are a popular filler and like all the other animal-derived products often associated with quality. As soft as a feather pillow may be or as warm as a down jacket may make you feel, nothing can justify the practice involved in plucking a goose (or any other bird) alive – a standard practice that hardly needs much explanation. It is exactly what it sounds like, pulling out the feathers of an animal that is forced to endure this painful procedure. Not surprisingly, the somewhat sensitive modern consumer is often soothed by producers with labels that guarantee the use of feathers from dead animals only. Similar to the discussion we had about the leather industry above, here the death of an animal is sold as a positive thing because the standard practice of live torture seems even worse. But even with this "better version" you need to accept the fact that birds had to die for your jacket. Again, this may have made total sense in a day and age when the alternative of pillow fillings was straw, but today we can create all kinds of soft materials. Think about it that way: If you are still caught up in the myth of leather, wool and feathers being these superior materials, then why do we use synthetics pretty much everywhere where performance truly matters? Performance gear is way more vegan-friendly on average than "regular" fashion, exactly because there the performance of the fabric matters more than just how it looks or feels on your skin. We can now produce high-tech materials that are lighter, warmer, softer – whatever you desire – than what cavepeople had available in nature.

Performing animals

The entertainment sector is another problem if we want to protect animals from human abuse. I am not even talking about the most obvious forms of abuse, such as dog fighting, cock fighting or similar. That is so plainly wrong that it hardly needs any comments. But actually, most "sports" involving animals are highly questionable. Every time we need an animal to perform in a certain way, especially under the pressure of monetization, we are probably not really acting in the animal's best interest. Animals that need to race are often only of worth to the owners as long as they can perform at their highest level. Afterwards, they are no longer of economic value and are often prematurely put down, also because injuries are not uncommon in bodies that have been pushed to the limit for a long time. Do horses want to be ridden? I never asked one, but I doubt it. I know, passionate horse riders will be quick to point out that a horse would not do the things they do (like jumping over high obstacles) if they were not perfectly happy with their human companion. But honestly, I call BS here. I never saw a horse approaching a human kneeling down, like "come, jump on my back, it will be fun!" and the horses I see occasionally grazing outdoors somehow never seem to jump around very much on their own, especially not over the fences around them. Just because an animal tolerates something and is cooperative, does not mean that it "enjoys" it or that it is in its best interest. But I'm not a horse expert, I just wonder what's in it for the animal. Circuses with animals go in the same direction. Not only do these animals have to perform a lot of tricks that are not exactly natural behavior, but by default, they also will spend a lot of time in small cages and traveling around. Behind closed doors, you can expect a fair share of well-documented abuse by trainers hitting the animals to force them into performing certain tricks or reported drugging of animals to make them more complacent.[31,32]

Zoos

The ultimate animal entertainment venue of course are zoos. Everybody loves the zoo, it's such a nostalgic place where children get to experience all kinds of animals firsthand. I remember days at the zoo as a particular highlight in my childhood. Observing animals I usually wouldn't see in nature was always exciting and I would go through rolls of camera film on every visit. But there's something very ironic about how we as a society perceive zoos. I remember all too well that while I was simply impressed in my childish innocence by the animals that I saw, my parents would see things that I didn't. They felt pity for the apathetic polar bear pacing up and down the few meters of space it had from one wall to the other. Yet it's the parents who bring their children to these places, thus supporting the very institution putting the polar bear into its state of misery. Granted, there are zoos and zoos. Some offer bigger cages, some offer smaller cages. The obscenely small cages for big animals are not even worth addressing and cannot be justified by any means. An orca whale does not belong in a swimming pool and neither does a polar bear. Some modern zoos have been doing better jobs at recreating bigger landscapes instead of classic cages but at the end of the day they are cages nevertheless and I would guess that ~~99%~~ 100% of the animals in a zoo, given the chance, would move around in a bigger radius than their cages permit. So what's the point of zoos? The most honest answer is probably entertainment. People love watching animals, that's why people go on safaris and that's why the internet is full of funny cat videos and that's why people go to zoos. But entertainment should not justify having an animal spend its entire life behind bars. Those who experienced a few weeks of lockdown at the peak of the corona pandemic in 2020 may remember how difficult it was not to leave your apartment, right? Now imagine some kids outside banging at your windows all day and making faces at you. That's what it's like for many animals at the zoo, only for a lifetime instead. Still not convinced by our double standards? Here's a fun experiment: Go to an online platform and let people know that you would like to have a cat as a pet but have it live indoors all the time. I promise you many emotionally loaded responses from outraged cat lovers, the same people who in all likelihood then bring their kids to the zoo on the weekend, where gigantic cats are trapped in cages. Zoos justify their existence with other motives, of course. They say that they are educational institutions and that they protect and preserve endangered species. I have serious questions about both motives. If a zoo is educational in the sense that it should teach us respect towards animals, maybe raise awareness for endangered animals in far-away places ("the ice caps are melting, save the polar bears!"), then I really wonder why it has such a low success rate? I mean, how much worse could it be without zoos? Given the amount of children that have visited a zoo in their lifetime, one should wonder why only a low single-digit percentage of adults decide not to eat the creatures they learned to protect? Maybe it's because even at the zoo you eat sausage in the restaurant for lunch after just having played with the goats? What kind of logic is that? We love animals, we want to save them, so let's kill them and eat them? Or are we only interested in protecting the "interesting" and "exotic" animals? Society gets watery eyes when they hear about rhinos being close to extinction because some people think their horns will give them a boner (or whatever magic power it is that they are supposed to possess), but it's perfectly ok to kill 1.3 billion pigs every year because people in definite need of magic rhino powder think it's masculine to throw a piece of pork on hot coals? If zoos

I can understand vegetarian, but vegan?

truly were schools, they should lose all their funding because I think their pupils are left in ignorance. What about preservation programs then? Isn't it nice that zoos try to keep breeding rhinos where nobody is hunting them? Yes, but at what price and with what success? First of all, only a tiny amount of the animals seen in a zoo are endangered.[33] There is no justification for locking up all the other animals because one endangered species might have a chance of preservation in a controlled setting. Second of all, the amount of money that is spent on infrastructure in modern zoos and the money they make every year equal preservation efforts of entire African nations in their national parks, where the animals can move freely, breed freely and repopulate in a healthy way.[34] I have not even mentioned problems of inbreeding, animals being drugged to calm them down or population control, which sometimes leads to perfectly healthy animals being killed for no other reason than them being "one too many" – as in the famous case in Copenhagen some years ago, when a two-year-old giraffe was shot, dismembered and fed to the lions.

Cosmetics and pharmaceuticals

There's another category of consumer goods where more animals and animal-derived products are involved than many may be aware of: the health and beauty aisle of the supermarket. I'm talking about cosmetics, shampoos, creams, pills and so on. On the one hand, many of these products have animal-derived ingredients in them that may not even be obvious from reading the label and are therefore off-limits for vegans. Want some examples? Shellac (comes from bugs), lanolin (comes from wool), collagen (comes from animal tissue), or cera alba (simply beeswax) are just a few of many ingredients that are animal-derived. If you don't want to become an expert on hundreds of chemicals, it's easiest to look for a vegan certification on the packaging. On the other hand, many of these products involve animal testing. I know we've come a long way and many countries have introduced stricter measures regarding animal testing, especially on non-medical cosmetics. But unfortunately, these are still full of loopholes and most brands need to test anyway if they want to sell in certain global markets. Vegans of course prefer their lipstick not to be tested on a rabbit. I also really hope that the cruelty behind animal testing needs no further explanation on why the animals suffer. Again, if you want to be sure, look for a label on the packaging, such as the "cruelty-free" or "leaping bunny" symbol.

The real concern on people's minds regarding animal testing is naturally "but so you don't take any medicine?" Again, we are talking about boundaries and people who are hoping to have finally found your weak spot where your moral high ground crumbles and where they can finally bust you for being nothing but an incoherent hypocrite yourself. Would I prefer if science was at a point where we could develop and test more (human) medicine without having to test it on other living creatures first? Definitely. I also do believe that animal testing could be significantly reduced if there were stronger incentives from funding institutions to move away from what currently is simply accepted standard practice and funding was redirected towards advancing new testing technologies. After all, it is often anything but clear that results from animal testing will be transferrable to humans.[35] So I'm sure that much testing could already be avoided. Technological innovation will give us even more options as time advances. But the status quo of today is that in order for me to get a life-saving treatment, more than likely some animals had to suffer and maybe even die in the process of getting that treatment on the market. And that's fully coherent with the vegan spirit. Remember that a vegan tries to avoid the suffering of animals "as far as practical and possible" not "over my dead body". Of course my interest in survival is above the interest of other animals, but quite frankly it's probably also above the interest of other humans. Or how many of you would voluntarily give your life for a random stranger on the street? If you would, congratulations, you are officially holier than a vegan.

So these are a whole bunch of reasons why vegans tend to think of vegetarians as "not quite coherent" when it comes to consequent non-participation in animal cruelty and why meat-eaters should not only question the consumption of their steak. In many ways, the dairy industry IS the meat industry, the egg industry IS the meat industry, the leather industry IS the meat industry. So any opposition to the meat industry automatically needs to include opposing these branches if we want to be somewhat consistent. A fair input now might be that even if you avoid dairy and eggs, it seems a bit "extreme" to read the label of every item you buy and not consume it because there is 0.5% milk powder in it. As a single item probably yes. But the bigger picture is that these cookies are not one item but produced in quantities of thousands and thus tons of milk had to be processed to end up being "just" that small trace of milk in one cookie. And most likely that milk was not the "local, organic milk, where all the cows are happy," but the cheapest industrial milk possible. Otherwise, you wouldn't be buying a cheap cookie for a few cents and somebody needs to buy all the mass-produced milk after all. I would therefore argue that the animal-derived ingredients present in tiny quantities in very commercial products probably are not the most ethically sourced versions thereof. Because no one pays attention. People may reach for the organic butter in the supermarket, but they probably won't question the origin of the butter that is listed among the ingredients in a cookie. So if we are concerned about the suffering of animals, the 2 grams of egg white present in the supermarket brownie might be even more problematic than the occasional local and organic entire egg, although the latter seems more substantial visually. That's why vegans bring the magnifying glass to the supermarket and get so annoyed when an otherwise perfectly vegan product is "tainted" with a seemingly pointless percentage of milk powder. Is it extreme? With all that knowledge now, you be the judge.

One final note on all the points discussed above. While I have mentioned that there are obviously individual exceptions to many of these standard industry practices, it

I can understand vegetarian, but vegan?

is also very important to be aware of a practice called "humane-washing". Humane-washing is the cousin on the more known greenwashing and works exactly the same only with a focus on ethical practices rather than environmental impacts[36]. Obviously no producer or seller of meat, milk, eggs, leather, cosmetics, etc. will advertise their products as being bad. Nobody will say "we sell the best mass-produced eggs and really only care about the price". Everybody instead claims their product to be produced with extra care. So with consumers becoming more and more conscious about environmental impacts or in this case the treatment of animals, it is also only logic that as a response we find more and more labels on consumer goods that suggest a particularly sustainable, fair, or "humane" production process. Think about it the next time somebody tells you that the animals from their meat producer are "slaughtered humanely". What does that mean exactly? Aren't these two terms in direct contradiction with each other? Just remember that we are constantly influenced by marketing and that reality is not always as it seems. Most people would probably be grossed out if they saw the actual animal behind their chicken nugget, a featherless zombie of a chicken. Industrialized production systems are as far removed from romanticized commercials as it gets.

Need more reasons? Your health and the planet

Still not convinced that you should go vegan? Your heart must be made of stone, but maybe your heart is the key to more selfishly motivated reasons: your health and your very existence. Personally, I never like to argue with people about health because for me it's not what veganism is about. And as I am not a medical doctor, I am in no position to give people health advice. I also fully acknowledge that it is possible to live a vegan life and live very unhealthy. French fries are vegan, so are plenty of potato chips, Oreo cookies, and many other junk foods you may crave. If these are your daily staples you can perfectly live a vegan lifestyle and perfectly ruin your health within no time. At the same time, it's no secret that most industrialized societies consume way more meat than health experts recommend and a switch to a "mainly plant-based diet" is advocated to combat some of our time's biggest health issues – cardiovascular diseases, obesity and diabetes.[37] Not too long ago, the WHO even categorized processed meat as carcinogenic.[38] So chances are that your body will thank you for going vegan in the long run. Even more important, we need to acknowledge that the planet we live on is in serious trouble (well, the planet is fine, we are the ones in trouble really). Food production contributes to a quarter of global greenhouse gas emissions! If we only look at methane, which is more potent than CO_2, agriculture is the biggest contributor. Think about this: livestock as a subsection of food production is alone responsible for almost 6% of global greenhouse gas emissions, without even factoring in deforestation. In comparison, global aviation, all the planes in the air, only make up less than 2%![39] Not surprisingly, a recent Oxford study said that a vegan diet is "the single biggest way to reduce your impact on planet

I can understand vegetarian, but vegan?

Earth".[40] You can do the math on almost any staple food and will find that plant-based alternatives beat out animal-derived food across the board, be it CO_2 emissions or water consumption, per gram or per calorie.[41] Beef alone is responsible for almost half of tropical deforestation and thus the number one driver of rainforest loss![42] If you now feel inclined to yell out "but avocados!" or "soybeans kill the amazon!", please stay calm and wait until we deal with the bullshit-bingo in chapter five. But regardless of how you feel about avocados, by going vegan, you will definitely help this planet to be much more inhabitable for yourself, your children and your children's children. With your food choices, you actually have a significant impact beyond the cute but mainly symbolic actions that we partake in to feel like we are doing our part. Or as a popular meme making fun of plastic straw bans eloquently puts it: so you'll stop using straws to "save the fish" but you won't stop eating fish to "save the fish"? *Confused smiley face*

Understanding Vegans

4   So what DO vegans eat?

After having talked about all the things that vegans choose not to eat, consume or engage in, we should probably also talk about what we do eat, as this seems to be a real concern in the public's perception. If you have never faced a situation in your life where you had to actively deal with your food choices and then a vegan comes along and tells you that meat, dairy and eggs are off the table, I can understand that it can probably sound a bit like there won't be much left to eat. But, for a long-term vegan, the question "what do you eat" is really hard to answer because, well, where to start? We eat as many meals as you, multiple times a day, and definitely not just tofu for every meal or nothing but salads. I can reassure you that there are plenty of foods left and if we can't give a simple answer to that question, then it is more due to the difficulty of summarizing 365+ meals in one sentence rather than the fact that there is nothing left for us to eat. But let's start in fact with vegetables. The vegetable kingdom is incredibly broad once you start to get acquainted with it beyond the identical three or four staple veggies that you carry home from the supermarket every week. Try some new things and you might just discover how satisfying vegetables can be, sometimes as simple as just throwing them in the oven with some olive oil and salt. Some of the world's best chefs have started to cook plant-based, so I guess there must be more to the vegetable kingdom than the brussels sprouts you didn't like so much as a kid. But I'm not saying that all you can eat now comes straight from the farmer's market. Pasta, rice, legumes, grains, flour, basically all the staples found in kitchens around the world are vegan and can be turned into an unlimited amount of amazing meals. And if you do crave a non-vegan item that you are used to eating, it is now easier than ever to replace that with a vegan alternative. In my home country, being vegan ten years ago meant finding one obscure tofu in the supermarket, everything else had to be bought in more specialized health food stores. Now the choice in regular supermarkets is overwhelming and constantly growing, shopping as a vegan has literally never been easier. A whole plethora of plant-based milk, cheese and meat replacements are available and allow you to recook occasionally a meal in a style you may be accustomed to. Please note, I'm not saying you HAVE TO eat Beyond Burgers and the likes. It's an option if you miss the taste of a burger. Somehow non-vegans always seem to be very concerned about vegans trying to imitate "their foods" when they start arguing in the comment sections of interactive media outlets. "Just eat vegetables if you don't want to eat meat!" I mostly do, thank you. However, since I'm not abstaining from meat for reasons of taste, but rather because I'm concerned about how a cow is becoming a burger, where is the harm in recreating that taste experience sans cow? But apparently, it's not only the fake meat we don't get concession for but also the imitation of shapes. "Why do vegans have to make their food look like meat (cheese/eggs/…) if they don't want to eat meat (cheese/eggs/…)?" Well mainly because nobody has invented triangle-shaped buns yet, so round burgers just fit better. Just kidding. But every time I get that question, I can't help but wonder – does that mean you believe that a sausage, a nugget, a burger or even a steak for that matter is a natural shape of an animal? You do realize that these are invented shapes for reasons of convenience!? The answer to the shape concern is simple: substitutes are made to look like the "original" exactly because they are supposed to provide a similar or even identical eating experience. I guess the marketing department over at Tofu Inc found out that people who have been eating animals ground and pressed into the shape of phalluses all their lives are more likely to switch to Tofu if they also make it look like a penis. Besides, instead of being upset about vegans making cashews look and taste like cheese, shouldn't the question be reversed? Shouldn't we be asking ourselves as a society why the hell we still kill chickens to eat nuggets, when we have advanced to the point where we can produce something that tastes exactly the same from soybeans, peas or wheat? It's a bit like people clinging on to coal energy. Why would you still burn coal if we can get the same energy from sunrays or the wind, etc.? Times change and they are changing fast.

Understanding Vegans

I feel like I need to open up a parenthesis here about the taste of "imitation items", especially because the most frequent concern I get from people is "I could never give up cheese" combined with a clear idea that vegan cheese tastes like cardboard. Granted, ten years ago, the very few alternatives that were available mostly did. But I promise you that nowadays you will find alternatives that are so close to some of the originals that it's really hard to tell them apart. Will they taste 100% identical if eaten side by side? Maybe not, but usually close enough to fool unbiased people. In addition, taste and preferences are acquired, not innate. What I mean by that is that you might for example have the idea that milk in your coffee tastes perfectly neutral and then experience on that first attempt at oat milk a prominent grainy taste. That's because you are used to how milk tastes, not because it is actually neutral in taste. So what at first might feel like an off-flavor can very quickly become the new normal. Just think about how you (probably) did not like alcohol or coffee as a child and then (probably) learned to like it as an adult. If you have been drinking oat milk for a while or nibbled on cashew cheese on a regular basis, it will no longer taste unusual. You might also actually even prefer it! Imagine for example how cheap industrial ham can have this flavor of pig (duh) that even meat-eaters often don't fully enjoy. Now a plant-based ham replacement may have a similar smokey flavor and texture minus the negative notes. Win-Win! Or we just accept the fact that replacements don't need to be 100% identical. Coke and Pepsi are more or less the same things, but then again they clearly are not. There's really no need to disregard one of them for having its own recognizable identity. But if one day you learned that one of the two companies was involved in a horrific business practice, you might be willing to switch to the other for reasons other than taste, no? Parenthesis over.

There is no fixed answer to the question "what do vegans eat" simply because the choice is so vast and personal preferences differ. If you think that vegans only eat salad and tofu, you mastered the creativity level of the average professional chef of the year 2010. But before starting my rant on restaurants, I would like to stay for a moment with the amazing variety of dishes found around the world that are vegan or easily made vegan. Just look for traditional local recipes and most cultures will offer real treasures. Why? Because most parts of the world didn't even have a dairy industry for most of their history and because meat used to be an expensive luxury. Eat what people used to eat when times were tougher and you will find some true gems in my experience! They are almost always full of simple and pure flavors and relatively easy to prepare. Did you know that the original pizza, called "Pizza Marinara," does not even contain mozzarella and is simply a combination of perfect dough with rich tomato sauce, garlic, olive oil and oregano herbs? So no, you do not need to substitute everything with fake replacement ingredients, just be open to learning new recipes and dive into exciting flavors from around the world! From Asian noodle dishes to Mexican bean tacos, Indian curries, or Middle Eastern mezze, the world is full of flavor without the need of harming any animals. And that's already talking about entire meals. You don't need to reinvent every snack of the day – ideally you already indulge in the occasional apple or any other fruit of preference as a non-vegan, so just keep up the good work and snack on!

If you are so inclined and prefer the occasional (or daily) "sin", you will now literally find everything in vegan-friendly versions all around you (granted, at least if you are connected to urban areas or shop at well-stocked supermarkets – but if you live very rurally, you will be used to some limitation of choices also as a non-vegan). It's hard to imagine a city where nobody has come up with a store selling vegan baked goods yet. Or the offering has already been incorporated by the big players anyway. Ten years ago, I had to fly to New York to find a vegan donut from a specialized craft bakery (yes, I did some sightseeing too), whereas in the meantime, the international chain Dunkin simply veganized much of their donuts in many European outlets for everyone, so I can now buy a vegan donut practically in front of my doorsteps. What a time to be alive.

Finally, let me introduce to you a few items that tend to crop up in vegan recipes and may not be part of your familiar repertoire (all in the spirit of helping you understand vegans). Especially those looking to substitute meat on their plate often take a page out of the Asian ~~playbook~~ cookbook and use tofu. Did you know that tofu is not even a meat substitute per se, but an independent food item on its own that in the Japanese cuisine is often combined with meat in one and the same dish?

Technically, it's more of a cheese anyway, given the resemblance of the production technique. You could say it's a soybean-based cheese. And yes, you should marinate it, just like you wouldn't eat chicken without any spices, herbs or marinades either. Tempeh is another soybean-based item that can be used instead of meat and is particularly popular in Indonesia. It's coarser in texture and maybe a bit of an acquired taste. I like to crumble it for a minced meat use. Seitan (not to be confused with Satan – unless you are gluten intolerant) is compressed wheat gluten with a similar consistency to meat. Jackfruit is a tropical fruit that if harvested unripe and grilled in a pan takes on a consistency similar to pulled pork. Moving on from the "meats," aquafaba is the fancy name for the liquid in a can of chickpeas that you usually pour out, which can be used to create fluffy egg white. Nutritional yeast is what vegans use to introduce a cheesy flavor to some dishes and tiny seeds called Chia can be used as thickener and egg replacer in baking as they become all jelly-like when mixed with water. Again, you definitely don't have to use these products if you don't like them, you can perfectly cook without them. In fact, you don't "have to" do anything as a vegan – everything is a choice, your choice. What I mentioned here are more traditional or less processed alternatives that have been around for a long time. There are today many alternatives that may substitute the ingredient of your choice more authentically in terms of flavor or consistency than the ones mentioned above.

Eating out

Eating at home is by default the easiest place to eat vegan because you control what's in your fridge and assemble the menu yourself. Eating out can be a bit trickier. I'm saying this without trying to intimidate you because, even in restaurants, eating vegan is easier than ever. But you may want to plan a bit ahead. Here's why: if you go to a random restaurant that has been around since the 80s and still offers the same menu from the 90s, they most likely have nothing on offer that sounds even remotely vegan. Probably the same is true if you walk into most rural restaurants. In these places, even salads are garnished with cheese and bacon. So obviously the easiest solution is to avoid such restaurants altogether. If there are restaurants nearby that have vegan options on their menu, take initiative and try to get your friends or colleagues to eat there before the restaurant choice is even made. But you may find yourself in a situation where you can't and end up stuck in one of those not very vegan-friendly spots. Some restaurants will not be very flexible when it comes to spontaneous special requests and I don't blame them if they are not going to organize a specialized substitute for you on the spot in the middle of their busy lunch shift. Calling ahead and asking can be one option and many restaurants will be happy to prepare something just for you. Otherwise, you probably will have to curb your expectations and order what is often referred to as vegan survival food: a portion of fries or a simple salad. Most vegans probably don't mind if that happens once as an exception, but of course we appreciate choice and good food like anybody else. So if you take out a vegan friend for a meal, you will do us a gigantic favor if we don't need to fight with the waiter over the possibility to get some plain salad without dressing.

But how do you even know that a restaurant has vegan options? In your hometown, you will become an expert pretty quickly. Connect with vegan groups on social media, there are dedicated groups everywhere sharing the latest food spots. When you are not in familiar territory and especially when you maybe cannot even understand the language of the country you are in, the app "Happy Cow" is a real lifesaver! This community-based app lists vegan restaurants around the world and has led me to places I never ever would have found or heard about otherwise. Most restaurants also have their menus online these days, so simply checking the website can be a good idea. Many restaurants choose not to write the word vegan next to vegan dishes (because they fear that close-minded meat-eaters will be scared and never come back) but work with symbols, such as leaves, flowers, letters like a small "v", or similar. Sometimes it can get a bit confusing if the restaurant also labels vegetarian options with similar symbols, so keep an eye out for tiny details like "v+." Every time I see a menu with the symbols "vg" and "v" I always feel a bit like when you stand in front of a restaurant toilet with these artsy gender symbols, where picking the right bathroom door boils down to a matter of chance. Luckily, there is usually an explanation of the used symbols hidden somewhere on the menu. But as much as I understand restaurants' desire to avoid in-your-face vegan messaging on their menus, I really appreciate clear labels. Of course we could just simply ask somebody from the staff but this brings us back to creating situations in which the label "vegan" ends up on our forehead instead of on the menu, where it actually belongs. Like I mentioned earlier, it is not always in our interest to make everybody aware of our being vegan. Maybe because we simply don't want to have that conversation today with the person we're eating with or because we are well aware that we can come across as annoying to others if every time we order food we need to mention that we are vegan. Confusing labels force us to ask for clarification whether an item is actually vegan and clear labeling could make our lives much easier. Unfortunately, restaurant staff also does not always handle special orders very gracefully. Often they will bring food to a big table yelling out "who has the veeegaaan pizza??" in a way that even the people who did not pay attention to what you ordered inevitably will understand that you are the one who made a "strange" request. Even worse, when the staff feels entitled to make jokes or start discussing their opinions with you. I have been asked by restaurant staff if I wasn't planning on finishing the decorative leaves I left on the plate (intending that vegans should eat leaves) and once a waitress even started telling me stories about people she knew who were vegan and had health problems. And I'm not even saying that this happens with bad intentions, as I am sure many people are not aware of how it can feel to be singled out at a dinner table. I'm just wondering why ordering a vegan option in some places still seems to be cue for "let's make fun of that person!" I guarantee you that one out of ten waiters will bring you your vegan option with a funny joke like "and here's your steak". Haha, ha, …ha.

Another potential challenge can be the fact that even in times when veganism is more popular than ever, many people are not familiar with what it really means. In some countries, even vegetarian can be a concept that is not fully understood. I've been served soup with fish pieces in vegetarian restaurants and just because somebody understands that you don't want to have meat on your plate does not mean they also understand that it may be a problem for you if the broth is made from meat, fish or bones. Especially when the staff offers something from the menu that suspiciously sounds like it would normally include butter, eggs, or cheese, I tend to double-check with them if that item is really vegan. Often it will turn out that you were simply offered a vegetarian option because the staff maybe did not think of all the ingredients. At the latest when the staff is offering you their gluten-free option, your alarm bells should ring and you might want to double check if they know what vegan means. I'm sure I'm not the only vegan who occasionally has used the excuse of food allergies in restaurants to make sure the staff is attentive to what I am actually requesting. (But I didn't just tell you that, keep it to yourself.) Fortunately, the vegan movement is spreading at a pace at which many restaurants understood by now that it might be much simpler to replace the token vegetarian option with a vegan option as you can satisfy many more potential customers with much less effort. I always have to laugh when I find myself confronted with meal choices on long-distance flights on which they give you options of dietary restrictions that are so specific that I can't help but wonder if that is worth the hassle. Here are some choices of special meals you can order when traveling with the national airline of my home country: lactose intolerance, vegetarian Hindu, vegetarian Jain, western vegetarian lacto-ovo, western vegan, kosher meal, Hindu meal or halal meal. I'm not an expert on religion and hope not to offend anybody with my ignorance, but from my understanding of the underlying principles of what can be eaten in almost any religion, a plant-based meal should satisfy pretty much any restriction you may subject yourself to. So while I admire the work some of these airlines put in to make sure that you do get exactly your preferred combination of food items while jetting through the sky, I wonder why they don't make it easier for themselves and just offer a well-made vegan meal as a standard choice and tick the boxes of almost any special dietary requirement at once.

Coffee shops have already completed this consolidation in many places I go to. While some years ago it was pretty normal to have lactose-free milk as an option and maybe a soy ~~milk~~ drink as a second option, resulting in many opened and semi-used cartons, now many places just offer a plant-based ~~milk~~ drink (sorry, I did it again, most laws strictly forbid the use of the term "milk" for something that did not include a mother, except for coconuts, but I'm digressing) to satisfy all demands for no lactose and no dairy requests.

So what DO vegans eat?

But back to meals. Another challenge of restaurant staff not understanding what vegans want arises in my experience when they have too strict an idea of what vegans eat. I know, you think now that vegan is already strict, how can it be even stricter? Well, stricter in the sense that many seem to assume that vegans eat only special foods that other people don't eat, like tofu. Here's a scenario I've experienced many times in the beautiful country of Italy, where so many esteemed local dishes are vegan by default or easily veganized by simply not grating cheese on top: "Hello," or rather "Buongiorno!" "Do you have anything vegan?" You can then see the staff in their mind going through the menu scanning their offerings like a Google search for the keywords "tofu", "Beyond Burger" and "weird ingredients that we don't eat here", and then quickly come to the conclusion "no, I'm very sorry, vegan… nothing." If you then challenge the staff, asking if they don't have a simple pasta with tomato sauce, or various vegetable dishes (what is normally called "side-dishes"), maybe even a risotto, they suddenly realize "oh, of course! We can make you this and that, also a little bit of this, with a side of that." Vegan does not need to be complicated and most vegans do not want to eat tofu all day and enjoy a simple pasta as much as everybody else. I don't actually mind these exchanges at restaurants, I have to admit, because I always feel like maybe, just maybe, I reached one more person in this world with the idea that vegans are not difficult or weird per default.

The last type of ignorance (not in an offensive sense, but in a "not knowing" sense) regarding vegan requirements is what you encounter when the staff of a restaurant (but sometimes of course also friends or relatives who offer you food or invite you for dinner) asks you if it's ok if there is "just a little bit of cheese in it." Basically, they acknowledge understanding that you don't want something, but try to negotiate what zero really means. Probably this is something that many young vegans still living at home will also experience with their parents, who suddenly need to prepare different or separate meals for their kids. "There is just a little bit of butter on the vegetables, ok?" "I only put very little ham into the sauce, you can pick out the pieces." While I have my clear views on "just a little bit" that I've already expressed earlier when talking about small percentages of animal-derived ingredients in supermarket products, it is directly leading to another subject that I do agree is not so clear cut. I definitely do not want "a little bit of ham" in my food. It would not kill me, but I am at a point where I do find it disgusting to chew on a piece of meat, both mentally and from a taste perspective. But, unless you go to a specialized vegan restaurant you cannot expect that all the meals you receive have been prepared in dedicated pans and grills, with zero cross-contamination.

Not too long ago, a big international burger chain (not the yellow arches, the other one) launched a vegan burger with the patty of the so-called Impossible Burger. It caused a lot of stir on social media among vegans, but not so much because of the excitement that another hugely influential fast-food chain has added a vegan option, but because word got out that they do not grill the vegan burger patty on a separate grill, but together with all the other (meat) burgers. So it quickly became a heated topic: would you go eat the new vegan burger, yes or no? Now the question of whether a food item is vegan if it has had contact with non-vegan ingredients is one to be answered by everybody individually first and foremost. I see how this is an entirely different question when we talk about certification – you may have already seen vegan logos on food packaging that certify a product as vegan friendly. They have clear guidelines that need to be followed for a product to be certified vegan and often the exclusion of potential cross-contamination is one of them. This may distinguish a product that is certified vegan from a product that according to the ingredients list looks vegan but comes with a warning that the product "may contain traces of" milk, eggs, shellfish or something like that. For most vegans, these warning labels are not a problem. They indicate that a production facility also handles the mentioned ingredients, cannot guarantee that there was zero cross-contamination and therefore want to make sure that people with severe allergies don't accidentally end up in the hospital. Most vegans will gladly eat the chocolate that "may contain traces of milk" as long as milk is not one of the listed ingredients. But of course you assume in this case that you are not actually eating milk, it's more a hypothetical possibility. A vegan burger happily frying away in a mixture of animal grease and blood from the beef burger right next to it is of course another level of contamination. I get how most vegans choose not to eat that patty and I would count myself as one of them. That

Understanding Vegans

is if I explicitly have been made aware of it like by the social media representatives of the folks over at burger royalty. The problem is of course that you never really know what's going on behind closed doors of a restaurant kitchen and I'm sure I've eaten my share of dinners that were prepared on the same pan or even fried in the same oil as some non-vegan products. But again, it's up to you where you draw the line and set your boundaries.

If you've now been patiently waiting for a rant on restaurants as I promised earlier, then these last few lines about eating out are for you. Maybe you already understood that from time to time it can be a bit frustrating going to restaurants as a vegan. And from time to time I really can't help but wonder how people ended up in their professions. If you earn your living by working in a restaurant and you have no idea what vegan means, then I cannot help but wonder whether you do have a minimal interest in the food industry? Have you been sleeping for the past ten years and just blindly served fries and chicken nuggets day in and out? Now don't get me wrong. Generally speaking, I agree with the idea that a restaurant does not have to cater to all the weird requests that people have if this is not their area of specialty. If you don't have fries, then you don't have fries, no problem. If you are a steakhouse, I most likely will not visit you in the first place, but I definitely wouldn't give you a bad review for not having tofu on the menu. But if you are one of these generic restaurants that serve a bit of everything and do not manage to come up with a single vegan-friendly option, you definitely missed the sign of the times. And if you decide to put a vegan option on the menu, please make just the tiniest effort necessary and create something "interesting." A vegan option is not a "normal" dish with things removed and a fruit salad is not a vegan dessert. I mean, it is a dessert and it is vegan per default, but it's not what most vegans want to eat for dessert. Why? Because that's what we get everywhere! Every friend we visit, every family dinner, it's always fruit salads! And I know that's not their fault. They may not be familiar with the idea of baking without eggs and milk, but a trained chef should definitely have better ideas than chopping up some fruit. Don't be obvious, surprise me! If you bring me anything other than a fruit salad, I will come back and order dessert again. The same goes for all the meals of course. A plain green-leaf salad for starters is not a "vegan option", it's something that should not be on the menu for anyone. Be creative, you're a chef for God's sake. Rant over.

What do (some) vegans (not) eat

Chances are that you may have come across news pieces where they write about "surprising items" that are not vegan friendly, like a list of things most people maybe wouldn't expect to contain animal-derived ingredients. Many people are very surprised to hear that wine or fruit juice is not always vegan-friendly. That's because these products are often processed with animal-derived substances that don't end up on the label. For instance, to clarify wine, fruit juices, vinegar, sometimes also beers, etc., manufacturers will often use egg white. The particles in the liquid will stick to the added egg white and can then be filtered out easily, rendering the liquid clearer. There will be no egg white in the drink afterwards, but vegans may choose not to consume these products anyway, because of course also the egg whites for wine filtration were produced by chickens, regardless of whether they end up in your drink or discarded beforehand. You may be even more surprised or straight-up grossed out that instead of egg whites some wineries opt for fish bladder. Also these practices are luckily more and more a thing of the past but in many industries, it is not yet established practice to declare vegan-friendly products as such, which is another reason why we are such good detectives. But jokes aside, animal-derived ingredients can be hidden in the most unlikely places. Apparently, many sugar refineries use bone char to make sugar white. Who would ever think of such a thing!? Learning about all of these things can be a bit overwhelming because it may seem like there are animal derivates hidden almost everywhere you look (or shop). But the reality is that most vegans do not stress out too much. Again, referring back to the definition of veganism and the whole feasibility aspect of it, let's keep in mind that none of us are looking for perfection. It may almost be an impossible task to eat out avoiding sugar everywhere you go and finding out if the sugar used in your dishes is vegan-friendly is definitely an illusion. Personally, I handle most of these cases along the lines of buying what I know to be safe (i.e., vegan-friendly) and ordering whatever is available. Meaning that if I buy a bottle of wine to consume at home, I will buy brands that

So what DO vegans eat?

I know to produce vegan-friendly, whereas I don't worry about it in a restaurant where no declarations are available. But that's really up to you. There are no 10 commandments and the police will not come to your house for routine tests. Probably some of your peers will poke at you a bit every time they hear about something somewhere that is not strictly vegan-friendly, all in the good spirit of sticking it to the annoying vegan who does not even play by their own rules. I'm always happy to learn, I'm sure I have not yet reached the limit of hearing about all the areas where human ingenuity came up with ideas to use parts of dead animals. I still find it funny though when people who actively engage in something objectively harmful as the killing of animals try to poke holes in your behavior if you TRY to do a good thing and avoid suffering and harm. "HAHA, sucker, you are also causing harm!" Yes, thanks. Unfortunately, I am. But veganism is an attempt to minimize it rather than simply accepting it.

Understanding Vegans

5 Deserted islands, lions and avocados

The time has come to play some bullsh*t bingo. Well, we're not actually going to play it, I'm just walking you through the bullsh*t arguments. If you are not familiar with BS-bingo, you basically have a bingo board where the numbers are replaced with keywords or short phrases that you expect in a conversation to come up and you try to complete the board. Great fun! Anyway, the reason this game works so well is that if you are familiar with a topic to a point where you talk about it frequently, you quickly realize that people arguing against you will always come up with similar arguments. Some of these arguments may be legitimate concerns, others are just pure BS. And trust me, there is a loooot of BS out there when it comes to arguing against veganism. So without further ado, and without further profanities, I present to you some of the most frequent arguments you will hear against veganism and my responses to them.

If we are not supposed to eat meat, why do we have canines?

Biologically speaking, humans are omnivores. That is a biological fact, not a matter of opinion. That means we CAN eat everything from plants to meat, but we don't necessarily HAVE TO. Whereas pure carnivores and pure herbivores are biologically dependent on nutrients from the respective food source and also have digestive tracts optimized to handle either green stuff or dead flesh, omnivores are much more flexible in their choices. As long as you meet your nutritional needs, you will survive either way. Now I know, especially us men tend to have this innate cockiness that we look into the mirror and see ourselves as Brad Pitt when in reality we probably are more of an Average Joe, but canines, really? Have you seen the teeth of a cat? Unless you are Dracula, those are NOT the same canines and I promise you, you will have some serious difficulties tearing through the skin and flesh of a cow next time you go out on a hike and your "carnivore instincts" take over. Those pathetic canines are not forcing you to eat animals, they help you work your way through a tenderly cooked piece of meat at best and serve just as well to bite into an apple.

But lions kill to eat meat, so why shouldn't I? It's all part of the circle of life.

Newsflash: You are not a lion! You are a human being, currently reading a book and therefore apparently somewhat capable of reflecting on your actions. Besides the fact that we just established that lions are biological carnivores, whereas you are not, they do not have the capabilities to go like "Hey Harry, ever thought about the fact that gazelles are suffering when we kill them? Maybe we should eat tofu instead!" We humans have the unique gift that we can analyze, philosophize, moralize, make rules for the world we live in, both in the interest of ourselves and the people living around us. That's why we also agree that, at least in theory, we should not have wars, kill one another, steal, rape, etc., etc. Animals don't hold climate conferences to save the planet. They don't have any responsibility or accountability for their actions. We do.

Humans have been eating meat for thousands of years!

True. But what does this have to do with what we are doing now? People who feel entitled to eat meat because "we've always done it" probably argue on the grounds of it therefore being natural, cultural heritage or evolution. We will encounter the argument that veganism is not natural again a bit later here. So to keep it short, we do many things that are not natural on a daily basis and condemn things that are natural (as in occurring in nature) such as war, murder, rape, etc. because we came to the agreement that they are maybe not our most favorable behavioral traits. Justifying animal exploitation on the grounds of cultural heritage means you must also be an avid supporter of bullfighting, whale hunting, eating cats and dogs, or if we extend it to humans, genital mutilation, forced marriage of minors, etc. Generally speaking, "we have been doing it forever" is hardly ever a good measuring stick for what's ethical behavior in a modern world. Last but not least, you often hear that we evolved only the way we did because of meat consumption. The argument goes that our brains were only able to grow as much as they did due to animal proteins. Although this theory has been challenged in very recent research,[43] for the sake of the argument, let's assume this to be true. Again, I have to ask how this is relevant to our present existence? It may have well been necessary in the past to hunt animals for survival and if this helped us get to where we are, good. But now we can maintain our current existence very well without eating animals and consuming animal derivates. Our brains are not going to shrink back to cavepeople dimensions, I promise. We now have supermarkets and most of us luckily need no longer worry about where and when the next opportunity for food will present itself.

I don't care about animals...

You clearly do not have to love animals to grant them rights or respect. There are many humans I don't care about very much. In fact, there are many emotions we all can have towards other humans, many of them negative. But this does not influence my acknowledging of basic human rights. I don't need to care much for other people to understand that the reason we all grant those rights to others is that we also want them for ourselves. We understand what it means to suffer and therefore agree that others should not be allowed to hurt us, while in return we don't hurt them either, no matter how little we care for them. All it takes is a tiny portion of empathy to put yourself in the shoes of an animal that has very similar interests. They don't want to get hurt, they don't want to suffer, they don't want to die. I can acknowledge that and grant them these interests without loving them or caring about them.

If you were on a deserted island, stranded with a pig, wouldn't you eat it?

Of course I would! I would also eat you if I were stranded on a deserted island with you. But guess what, we aren't, so I don't need to worry about that and neither do you because I can go get my food at the supermarket and don't need to go Hannibal Lecter on you.

Where do you get your protein from?

From the same place where your steak gets its protein from. Plants. It's interesting that protein gets so much attention from non-vegans, although it is hardly among the top nutrients you might potentially be on the lookout for as a vegan. Even more interesting is the image that exists around protein, strength and masculinity, given that some of the strongest animals on the planet like elephants or rhinos build up all their strength and mass with nothing but plants. Be that as it may, there is this myth that we need animal-based proteins to survive because they are "complete proteins," meaning they contain all essential amino acids that our body cannot produce itself. There are however also plant-based sources of complete proteins, such as soybeans or hemp seeds, but there's no need to worry about complete proteins in the first place. Our body can readily combine the essential amino acids from different meals and get all the protein it needs even if we don't eat all those essential amino acids together at the same time.[44] So protein is really nothing to be concerned about. But if you do want to know some fantastic vegan protein sources, look no further than legumes! That's lentils, chickpeas (Mmmm, hummus!), beans, peas, in all shapes, sizes and forms. Also, more and more professional athletes switch to a vegan diet and still manage to excel at the highest level. So if they can do it, you can do it as well, no matter how "physical" your job or your hobby is.

Avocados are bad for the environment, soybeans destroy the Amazon, vegans are killing the planet!

I think the avocado idea started with one of these badly researched articles from an online news site that had a catchy title like "vegans are killing the planet" and then was shared thousands of times by super excited meat-eaters who could finally stick it to their annoying self-righteous vegan friends. I too was devastated when I learned that I can no longer start my day with avocado toast. Obviously, that is a load of crap. These articles exist in various forms, sometimes with other foods like quinoa, but the argument goes always along the lines that the food in question uses a lot of water to grow or is transported very far and thus really bad for the planet. Besides the fact that transportation is basically a non-factor for the carbon footprint of individual foods, but also in terms of the average diet,[45] and that water use is overall highest for animal-derived foods,[46] I have no problem admitting to the reality that individual (vegan-friendly) food items can have bad environmental footprints. Also almonds are part of that group. But who said that vegans live from nothing but avocados and quinoa? I cannot even remember the last time I ate quinoa! According to that logic, vegans ditch meat, dairy and eggs and replace them with avocados and quinoa. If that were the case the vegan diet would obviously be pretty boring. Not with a single word do these articles mention the fact that also non-vegans eat avocados and that they are not substitutes for the items we exclude in our lifestyle. We need to compare things that make sense, of course. If we replace meat with tofu or dairy milk with oat drink, the ecological benefit of favoring plant-based choices is massive! And no, just because you are vegan you do not have to eat exotic fruit or learn how to cook quinoa.

Another myth is the soybean problem. Telling people that meat and dairy are bad for the environment really seems to strike a nerve because I hardly know anybody who will admit to this truth without trying to immediately poke holes in the vegan food chain. My favorite? Soybeans destroy the Amazon. It is true that soy production taken together with palm oil is the second-largest driver of tropical deforestation – although making up still less than half as much as the biggest driver, the beef industry. But, it is much more important to understand what this soy is produced for. Of the global soy production, only 6% is used for direct human consumption such as tofu or soymilk, whereas almost 90% is used for animal feed, mainly for poultry and pigs. So it's not tofu eaters that drive deforestation, but industrial meat farming.[47]

I once knew a vegan who was sick after a month and now eats meat again.

And I know, not personally, but through statistics, 1.6 billion meat-eaters worldwide who suffer from overweight and obesity.[48] Obviously, there are sick vegans, just like there are sick meat-eaters. And, like I said earlier, you obviously cannot expect to thrive on a vegan diet if you only eat chips or drink nothing but smoothies all day. But I always found it very interesting that when I was having coke and burgers for almost every single school lunch in my youth, nobody was worried about my health. Go vegan and everybody around you becomes a doctor in nutrition. Just like some smokers live healthy lives into their nineties, there are health food advocates who die young. Let's trust broader statistics rather than anecdotal evidence to make sound decisions on what works and those numbers say that you will not die from switching from dairy to oat milk.[49]

Plants feel pain too!

I've already addressed this earlier and I really have a hard time believing that anybody seriously argues that plants are the same as animals in their capacity to suffer, so my first reaction is usually trying to figure out if this is a serious concern or if I am just dealing with a troll. Besides the fact that plants clearly do not have the same capacity to suffer as animals – no brain, no nervous systems, no capacity to flee, etc. – eating animals is even worse if you are truly worried about the feeling of plants. A cow needs to eat much more plants for you to eat a piece of the cow than if you ate the plants directly. So please reduce plant suffering and eat them directly yourself.

Eskimos need to eat meat to survive!

This might be true or the reality for a handful of isolated communities in the world. Some indigenous people, hunter-gatherer communities in remote parts of the world, or small tribes that live almost completely cut off from the modern world as we know it may indeed rely on hunting for survival. Now I don't know about the Eskimos in particular, and to be honest, I am too lazy to do research on whether a Starbucks has already opened up in the Arctic or not, but for the sake of it, let's assume they fully depend on hunting for survival. Fine. No vegan is going to take that away from them. But you don't rely on hunting and the vast majority of people on this planet do not either. I'm happy to repeat that in cases of life or death most vegans would gladly choose to live and kill for their own survival. But if it's not a necessity, then what's the justification? It's never a good moral compass to justify your own behavior by simply pointing at others. That's how the world works for 4-year-olds ("But they do it too!"), to which the more intelligent parent usually responds oh so wisely, "so if all your friends jump off a bridge, are you going to do it too?"

You should worry about more important things, like human suffering!

Prioritizing where your time, money and attention are directed to makes absolute sense of course. But this common reaction towards veganism starts with a false premise: Who says that somebody advocating for animal rights does not care about human rights? I could be particularly picky now and point to the fact that also humans are animals, so veganism by default includes the non-suffering of homo sapiens. I am yet to meet a vegan who doesn't care about the mistreatment of humans. We tend to be quite a friendly bunch, all in favor of peace, love, kindness and equality, even if some of us may get a bit feisty when fighting in the name of those without a voice. But at the end of the day, veganism is probably the singlehanded biggest reduction of suffering in this world you can yourself enact on a daily basis. With every single meal you eat, you can choose death or kindness. You can choose a diet that can feed the entire planet or one that not only harms animals but destroys the planet for us humans, too. And yes, you can still fight against wars, human trafficking or whatever topic that is most important to you, one does not exclude the other.

Even if we think of animal rights advocacy more in the classic sense, with all the attention on four-legged creatures, veganism is more directly related to human issues than you might think. American slaughterhouse workers are reported to be three times more likely to suffer from serious injuries than the average worker[50] and are prone to mental health issues and antisocial behavior including forms of violence.[51] The widespread antibiotics use that is necessary to keep factory-farmed animals healthy is resulting in antimicrobial resistance and is considered a serious threat to human health.[52] We are literally jeopardizing one of the biggest medical advancements we've made if antibiotics no longer work as desired. And no matter what origin story of Covid-19 you believe in, it is clear that many dangerous viruses have been transmitted to us from unsanitary interactions with animals, so it is probably only a matter of time until the next pandemic will hit. Vegetables don't cause pandemics, wet markets "probably" do and definitely can.[53]

We can't even reach equality among humans, so what's the point of fighting for animals?

A popular variation of the previous talking point is the idea that if you can't do X then there's no point in doing Y. Of course that's a very lazy excuse and the easiest way not to get anything done ever. As the saying goes, "two wrongs don't make a right", so letting something inherently negative pass, just because there already is more negative existing anyway really just adds to the negativity. It does not matter where you start in the big picture, but if you can, do something! Doing nothing is the equivalent of just quitting everything. A world in which you maybe cannot prevent a war from happening but a pig gets to live is a better world than one in which the war happens AND the pig dies. It may not save all the problems in the world, but it's a start.

Humans are above animals!

There are various angles to this point of thinking. Biologically speaking, there is no such thing as a "crown of creation". Granted, in many things we are much better than other beings on this planet and those many things are mostly related to our capability to use language in a way no other life form manages to communicate. This allows us to reflect, plan, collaborate and negotiate in ways never seen before on this planet. So our brains are pretty cool. But other animals can change their color, are faster, stronger, live longer, can fly, whatever you name. Evolution brought about different strengths in different areas. Our "superpower" does indeed allow us to control what happens with the rest of the world around us and therefore puts us more or less in a position of domination over all other species. But with power comes responsibility. It is easy to be a bully, but only if you put yourself in the shoes of the bullied, you understand your power. Imagine aliens landed on our planet tomorrow. Imagine they were much more intelligent than us and quickly captured us all. Then they start to eat us because a) we taste good and b) just because they can – after all, they managed to catch us. Would you still argue according to the logic that the one in power can do whatever they want if you were the one that is about to be eaten? You probably would try to reason with them, saying that you want to live and that you suffer in the cages they keep you. Well, animals are telling you the same things if you listen to them – they may not have the language to tell it to us plainly, but they clearly communicate disagreement when you try to hurt them. Since we have other options, bully behavior is not a good look on us and power is a horrible excuse for doing horrible things.

Another angle to this is that vegans are often accused of believing animals to be exactly equal to humans. Because every time we make the comparison to humans, this implies equality. When vegans refer to eating meat as murder – because that is the term we would use if that cow was a human being – what people hear is "they think cows are equal to people." I definitely do not believe that we are equal in every regard, but we are similar enough in some relevant aspects, for example in our capacity to suffer. Of course I would save a human child in a burning house before I'd save the chicken – it is completely normal to protect your own species first. I would also save my own child before somebody else's. But that doesn't mean that the subject more distant to me has an equal worth of being saved in situations where I have the option to save more than just one of them. Simply put: animals are not more important than humans, but they are more important than a sandwich.

Veganism is a luxury problem!

If you are in a situation of pure survival, veganism might not be one of your top priorities. See also the deserted island argument. But that does not mean that people with lower incomes cannot eat a vegan diet. In fact, all of the most basic vegan staple foods, from vegetables to grains, legumes, rice, you name it, are by default some of the cheapest foods you can buy, whereas meat is much more expensive. Many of the most traditional dishes in any society are vegan-friendly exactly because the gardens and fields offered the most affordable foods in times of hardship and poverty. You do not have to eat beyond burgers to be vegan. If anything, it is a human-made problem that underprivileged communities do not have access to some vegan options. Dairy, for example, is highly subsidized in many countries and that is the main reason it is cheaper than many non-dairy alternatives. If you can buy beef for less money than a piece of tofu, then that is purely political. The true cost of raising an animal and then turning it into something you buy at the supermarket must be higher naturally speaking. If it isn't, it is only possible due to political decisions, corporate interest and the worst possible circumstances of factory farming with disastrous tolls on the environment that will have to be paid for later by future generations. Veganism is not only for influencers, hipsters and privileged people in suburbs but in the interest of everybody and feasible for everybody. The real luxury problem is that we forgot that our grandparents could afford to eat meat maybe once a week and we now think that we are somehow entitled to eat it three times a day.

Vegans should stop forcing their minority views on others, everybody has the right to eat whatever they want.

In an ideal world, I would like you to come to the conclusion yourself, for yourself, that killing animals is unnecessary and that vegan alternatives are the way to go. But here's the problem with freedom. (I'm all for it by the way – go freedom!). By definition, if we want freedom for everybody, then my freedom cannot go further than where it starts affecting your freedom. Classic smoker debate: You may have the right to smoke a cigarette whenever you want, but as soon as your smoke starts infringing on my right of not wanting to inhale your smoke, you can no longer claim a right of unlimited freedom, because I have the same right to freedom. So smoking all by yourself in your house, in your car, is absolutely your freedom, go nuts. But if you sit on a train next to me, I have the same right of not wanting to be exposed to your cigarette smoke and your freedom needs to be contextually limited to protect mine. What does that have to do with eating animals? Well, of course that depends on what rights you grant to animals. It can be argued quite simply that the right you claim to eating an animal pretty strongly infringes on the animal's interest or "right" to live, so technically your right or "freedom" would have to be limited in order to protect the animal's freedom to live. But I know, we live in a schizophrenic world where most advanced nations have explicit laws that protect animals from abuse so that we can punish people who mistreat their dogs for example. But somehow these rights become completely meaningless as long as we eat the animal after the abuse. So the freedom of choice debate is naturally centered around the legal status of animals and currently, you obviously do have the legal right on your side to eat a cow. Legality does not always entail morality, but that's another discussion.

There is another side to this topic, however. People who claim that what you eat is up to you ignore the reality that most countries already have laws that limit what you can buy and eat. They probably only don't realize it because their culture frowns upon the consumption of those products. There is a purely political reason why you probably do not find shark fins or whale meat in your country but can buy chopped-up octopus legs. But as most of us seem to care very much more about dolphins being hunted than about pigs being slaughtered, a legal limitation of what we can eat based on animal welfare is probably nowhere near. On the other hand, animal-based foods are a major contributor to climate change and thus to the destruction of the planet we inhabit. So modern food choices – to some degree – do need to be regulated for the simple reason of our own survival. If everybody on this planet just said "well it is my freedom to eat steak Monday to Sunday, three times a day," we could just give up on trying to stop climate change altogether, stop reproducing, fly to the Bahamas three times a year and enjoy what's left of this beautiful planet while it lasts. Of course, I'm being a bit overdramatic, but if we do care about the future, we cannot claim that our eating habits are not anybody else's concern, because, of course, they do concern all of us.

Oh and one last word on minorities "forcing their views on the majority." Somehow I get the feeling that people feel inconvenienced quite easily these days. Anytime a non-dominant group is asking for a change that would accommodate them, people get outraged. Whether it's a demand for linguistic change to be more inclusive for all genders or a simple request for a vegan option in the cafeteria, the results are always the same: "Don't force your food on me!" "I've been calling it such and such all my life!" "Why do we have to change things for a handful of people?" "Don't we have bigger problems!?" It's mind-blowing because more often than not those changes don't even affect the majority, they simply accommodate those who feel currently excluded, so where is the force? Do "we" have bigger problems? Maybe. Maybe you do. But for those who are actually affected, those small changes can make a big difference. For all the animals currently being slaughtered it certainly would make a big difference. And whether you like it or not, this is how social change works! People making demands for inclusion, equality and respect outside their own bubble of people who are already on bord. If slaves had not rebelled, if women had not spoken up, if the LGBTQ-community had not protested, we would still be living in a world with a lot more inequality and oppression. The disadvantaged absolutely need to make themselves heard! And since animals cannot reason with you that you should give tofu a try and spare their lives, it is up to animal rights supporters to deliver the message to you. If you don't want to listen, fair enough. But the world will change whether you like it or not. And vegans will never stop standing up for animals, that's for sure.

We need to hunt to control animal populations!

Ah yes, the good old tale of good-natured humans who do a kindness to nature by roaming the woods and liberating it from the terror reign of deer. The question is of course, why do overpopulations exist in the first place? The answer is because of hunting. In most cases, the reason that a particular species is growing in unusual proportions is human made. We extinguished natural predators like wolves in many of our forests, leaving other animals without natural enemies. Or we simply introduced the species ourselves, as it happened for example in Italy in the mid-1900s with wild boars. They were introduced from Eastern Europe, ironically so there would be more to hunt. Back then it was a good excuse to run around in forests in military gear, now it is responsible for 100 million dollars of agricultural damages every year.[54] Anyway, I find it hard to believe that if we really need to control deer populations, the only way to do this is to run after them with dogs and shoot at everything that moves. If we can perform life-extending surgeries on dogs, we should probably also be able to tranquilize and castrate a deer, but I guess the true answer is that we don't want to, not that we can't. Probably because deer genitals are much less decorative on restaurant walls than antlers.

Vegans need to take pills, this is not natural and therefore can't be good.

It is correct that there is one critical nutrient or vitamin that vegans need to pay particular attention to, namely vitamin B12. Vitamin B12 is formed by bacteria in the digestive system, so herbivores survive by synthesizing their own B12. Also humans apparently do produce B12, but in the wrong intestine for it to be absorbed – probably one of the features we can thank our meat-eating ancestors for.[55] Anyway, there is no way around admitting that today we rely on outside sources for our B12, so either by eating animals that synthesized B12 for us or by supplementing it. Since vegans prefer not to eat animals, they simply opt for the pill. Or drops or sprays or foods that already have been fortified with B12 like many brands of plant ~~milk~~ drink, for example. It's really not a big deal, it does not mean that vegans need to consume all kinds of weird supplements and medicines to stay alive.

Then there is the naturalism argument that supplementation is not natural. I assume that people who argue along these lines are the same people who refuse modern medicine because they like to live as naturally as possible. Of course they also don't use glasses to improve their sight and don't use cars or bikes to get from A to B, because none of these things are natural. They are inventions, advancements, successful discoveries, whatever you want to call them, that can improve our lives. We do not suddenly have a life expectancy that is pretty much double of what it used to be some centuries ago because we rely on nature. Nature can be brutal, so most of us willingly choose unnatural "help" to cure or improve what nature is doing to us. And since we're already here, it's also not very natural that commercial farm animals are way fatter, bigger, and more productive than they used to be, because we modified them for profit. It is also not very natural to take the flesh of an animal and shape it into nuggets, sticks and sausages, heck it is hardly natural to cook or grill meat in the first place! All other "natural meat-eaters" in the wild catch, kill and devour their prey raw.

Our animal protection laws are already very good. In our country there's no need to worry! Just buy local!

One of the benefits of a well-connected or "globalized" world is that you get to hear also what is going on in other countries, which, with a portion of open-mindedness, allows you to see some things in a broader context. Especially politics tends to fight local battles and understandably so. Politicians don't get elected by other countries and they are supposed to represent the interests of the local population. But that does not mean that all the problems we are trying to solve in this world are truly local. Improving something locally is definitely part of a global improvement, but a comparatively better situation should not be a reason to just ignore the problem until the rest has caught up. Just because a country has high standards in medical infrastructure and high overall life expectancy, it doesn't stop its medical research programs.

Progress for us can also mean progress for others: you can be a role model and you can export knowledge, experience and products to areas that have not been in the position to making this a priority. But let's be honest, whenever I hear the argument "oh we have some of the highest standards in the world" I can't help but smirk a bit in disbelief. Again, I grew up in Switzerland, one of the world's wealthiest nations, and our standards of living are through the roof. It's easy for somebody living here to believe an expert when they say "our standard of X is much higher than anywhere else." But funny enough I hear the same arguments coming out of the mouths of experts from almost every other country. I've seen documentaries about food production coming from many countries around the world. Funny enough, there is always a representative of a government agency or the meat industry smiling into the camera and claiming "oh we have some of the strictest laws for animal protection in the world". This is basically a way of saying "stop asking critical questions, other people are doing the bad stuff, you are fine, continue doing what you were doing." Obviously, it is not possible that all the countries have the highest standards while at the same time horrific pictures taken by activists are emerging out of farms and slaughterhouses in all these countries (including my own). And of course you can always go read the laws of your country if you really want to know. According to an independent ranking, Switzerland is indeed among the six leading countries with the highest animal protection standards,[56] but if this is as good as it gets, then we are naïve to believe that animals in captivity live a decent life anywhere on this planet. Oh and one final point: Next time you eat out, check the small print declaration to see how much of your meat and fish actually comes from abroad. Animal welfare is not better in any country as long as not equally strict rules apply for imported goods and are actually being controlled. But ethically speaking, it is a global problem anyway, just like human rights should protect people regardless of where they were born.

My actions will not make a difference anyway...

I know it's hard to see how one person's behavior should be relevant when we talk about billions of animals being killed. The easy answer is that if everybody thinks like this, we will never get anywhere. Many individuals together make up enough people to have serious impact. After all, we vote with our dollars, we create demand with what we consume. If enough people stop buying meat at the supermarket, this will inevitably lead to a decrease in production in the long run. Without demand, there is no production. With changing demand, there is changing production and that has become very noticeable over the past few years. Big meat corporations have started to produce also vegan alternatives and big dairy corporations have started to produce plant-based alternatives to milk, cheeses and yogurts. Why? Because demand has become big enough for it to be financially interesting for them, so they want a piece of the pie. At the end of the day, most corporations don't care so much what it is they earn their money with as long as their factories keep running and money keeps flowing. Especially since they already have the tools and infrastructure needed anyway. Also, your behavior will influence people around you. Your peers may not all go vegan as well, but you might just be the reason they will ever so often try a vegan option and learn a thing or two about veganism along the way. And that's where one becomes two, two become three, and eventually enough for consumer demand to bring about meaningful change.

But we can also look at this more philosophically, so to speak. Even if the link between my consumption and an animal's death may not seem imminent, it is plausible that every piece of meat I don't buy will eventually be one animal less that will get raised and slaughtered. While this still may look like little in the grand scheme of billions, it matters if we understand that animals are individuals, just like us. If I decide to rush a relative with a heart attack to the hospital, I'm also not doing this because it matters in the grand scheme of the billions of people who live and die on this planet. I do it because this particular individual matters. Because this person has a story, a life he or she clings on to, a subjective experience of life on earth. Nobody would say "oh what difference does it make" and just let the person die. Similarly, that one (or eventually many) animal(s) that you save by going vegan matters because it matters to THEM. Every individual counts.

We all cause harm through our existence and vegans kill animals too!

At the risk of sounding repetitive, veganism is not perfect and it does not have the goal of being perfect. We are well aware that through our sole existence on this planet, we inevitably use up resources and inevitably kill animals in doing so. But when we are accused of being hypocrites for "all the animals we kill" during crop harvest, then we are comparing apples and oranges. If our intention is to harvest vegetables and a mouse happens to get squashed by a truck, that is not the same thing as me intentionally killing the mouse. That's why you get a very different sentence if you deliberately run over a person than when that person ran unexpectedly in front of your vehicle. Intention clearly matters and there is no intention in killing animals while harvesting grains but a lot of intention behind the slaughter of an animal for its meat. Also, see the "plants feel pain" argument for a kind reminder that we are harvesting much more crops to first raise the animals we are currently eating, so by not eating meat, we also help the mice and other tiny animals in the fields.

We all just need to relax a bit more about food and enjoy life.

This is one of the most common lines of arguing that I come across in lifestyle sections of newspapers and magazines, when they write opinion pieces about veganism. Often they interview some kind of food professional, who will gladly accept that there are some truths behind the idea of veganism but ultimately rejects the idea as being too strict. "Food has become too political", "food has become a religion" and "we all just should relax a bit more" is a very typical conclusion. And I get it, we live in a day and age where every week a new study comes out that tells us what we should and shouldn't eat. Social media is full of advice on what's good and bad for you. We live in constant guilt because we work too much, don't move enough and don't eat healthy enough. But to claim that veganism is to be rejected for its strictness is kind of missing the whole point. Veganism exactly is not a diet. If veganism were only about living a healthy lifestyle, I completely agree that a less strict version of it would be just fine. But it's a moral question that we are being strict about. Saying that we should relax a bit more about animals being killed for our enjoyment is a bit like a police chief telling the officers to relax a bit about fighting crime. "Sure it's important that we catch thieves, but hey it's Sunday, they also want to have some fun, let's relax a bit and worry about it again next week!" The problem is of course that the current consensus in society is not the vegan one and therefore stopping to do what is accepted as normal is considered "strict". But also torture has once been considered normal and nobody really misses it today and thinks it's too strict that we no longer engage in a bit of occasional dismemberment.

Why is all this BS so predictable?

Psychology. There is a concept called cognitive dissonance, which basically describes the state we are in when our behavior does not align with our beliefs. This can occur in many walks of life, but eating meat is a very popular example of this as many (if not most) people who eat meat believe simultaneously that they like animals. This causes inner tensions that need to be resolved, for which we tend to use one of the following three strategies. Either we change our behavior and stop eating meat. Or we justify our behavior to ourselves by finding excuses why what we do is ok. Or we simply flat-out ignore any information that conflicts with our beliefs. With the latter, we get a lot of help from the meat industry itself because what's easier to ignore than something you don't get to see? Commercials don't show slaughterhouses and factory farms, but single happy (living) animals on green pastures. But it's the justification part that really explains all these typical objections that vegans get. When a vegan challenges your cognitive dissonance, you almost instinctively will come up with excuses that your behavior is normal, natural and necessary, whereas the challenger must be surely inconsistent in their behavior themselves (the deserted island), just as bad as you (avocados, killing plants and insects), or plainly wrong (veganism doesn't work, it's unhealthy). Ignoring and justifying conflicting information is of course much easier than changing your behavior, which is probably why only very few people actually make the switch and go vegan in the short run. But we are in for the long distance, we hope to get you there by chipping away at your arguments one by one, meal by meal, obstacle by obstacle. And who knows, maybe one day you will realize that it's not so outlandish not wanting to kill animals and consume what the plant kingdom has in stock instead.

Understanding Vegans

6 A vegan world

One can dream, right? Currently, vegans make up a percentage in the lower single digits of the global population. Although I'm convinced of the importance that moving towards a vegan diet will inevitably play in the near and distant future, I am not all too optimistic that we will be living in a predominantly vegan world anytime soon. But this is not a reason not to do your part. Maybe our grandchildren will one day look back in disbelief and wonder how we could ever raise billions of animals only to kill them again, to eat them, to wear them, or to try out if a lipstick will give you a rash. I certainly hope so. Even if that should not be the case, the idea of a hypothetical vegan world is on the minds of many people who are challenged by the idea of veganism. A vegan society is a concept so fundamentally different from anything we are living in right now that people inevitably wonder "how the hell is this supposed to work?" Is it really all that different though? I certainly don't think so because I have been living the vegan experience firsthand and don't see how my experience and existence could not be yours, your friends', your parents' or your children's experience as well. I am not living on another planet. I mostly shop for groceries in the same supermarkets. I go to restaurants on a regular basis. I enjoy tasty food and a good glass of wine in even better company more than anything else. I too believe that a leather jacket can look pretty fly and I certainly love observing animals. Only that I manage to achieve all these things for the most part without directly harming animals. And if I can do it, you can do it too and probably the majority of the world as well (except for the Eskimos). I promise that I do not have any superpowers and that I'm not living a withdrawn existence of hermitage somewhere in a forest. So yes, a vegan world is possible.

But still, there are some concerns on people's minds that we should address here. What exactly does a vegan world look like without all these farmed animals? Will they no longer exist? What about the farmers? Can we feed the world? Let's talk about it!

Superficially, a vegan world would look very similar. Most of the commercially farmed animals are invisible anyway, neatly hidden away in gigantic barns so people don't see them. If you live in a more rural area, there's a good chance you will see maybe some cows grazing on fields (those who are lucky enough to get to spend time on the pastures). But for the most part, you don't encounter chickens or pigs roaming around freely very much. Supermarkets would still be showcasing the same variety of items as ever, only some would be replaced by vegan alternatives. Already now I've been to supermarkets that have a bigger range of plant drinks than dairy milk, so no need to worry about empty shelves. Circuses would no longer have acts with animals but just as many clowns and acrobats as ever, if not even more. Zoos would disappear in their classic form, but animal sanctuaries, where rescued animals can live out a life under care, can still be a touchpoint for human interaction with animals you might not see every day. The real difference is that there could not be a commercial interest in keeping the same animals and/or breeding them – a sanctuary has "on offer" whoever happened to be in a need of shelter. Lots and lots of grassland that is unsuitable for vegetable farming could be reforested to increase biodiversity, to offer natural habitats for animals and for simply letting the planet heal from all our deforestation and land clearing. And then there are the farmers. What are we going to do with all these poor farmers that will be out of a job? Are vegans really so selfish? Well, yes and no. Parts of me have little sympathy for somebody who chose to build their livelihood on the suffering of others (this is the emotionally unhinged, f*** the world part of me). We constantly create circumstances that put certain job groups at a disadvantage. Not too many people care about the tobacco farmers when they advocate smoking bans. Who considers the thousands and thousands of employees at the big food corporations like Nestlé, Mondelez, Unilever, etc. when we tell our children that they shouldn't eat so many sweets? Ultimately, "but that's how I earn my money" is not a good excuse to justify my immoral business practice. That's why mafia bosses usually end up in jail and don't get unemployment benefits if somebody catches them selling drugs. But the more rational and understanding part of me will of course acknowledge that us vegans have nothing against farmers per se. I do believe that most farmers and vegans do share the same interests, only that most farmers were born into a system that is normal for them now but could easily be changed in the future. If you are a farmer, you can also farm vegetables, fruit or grains. You do not have to raise animals. Somebody will have to grow all the oats for a world full of oat milk drinkers and the tons of kale for green smoothies. Another fantastic point is made by vegan activist Ed Winters, who produces some of the best-researched content on veganism available both online and in his recent book: farmers are good at managing land and could receive the same government subsidies to manage land without animals on it, land that we can rewild for a better ecosystem.[57] So much land will be freed up if we remove the animals out of the food equation. Why? Because animals on dinner plates are such inefficient calories! The amount of soy you feed a pig to end up with one sausage is so big that we could eat maaaany more (soy-) sausages by skipping the pig in between. It is estimated that in the United States alone, an additional 350 million people could be fed if all animal-based items were replaced with plant-based options.[58] That's a staggering amount of extra food considering that the global population keeps growing and we need to find a way to feed all these people.

So what about all those animals then? Do vegans really want cows and pigs to go extinct? Ideally, no. Nobody wants animals to disappear from our planet. But let's be very clear about the fact that we created (in the sense of modified through breeding) animals that in most cases could not even survive in the wild. The sad reality is that most chickens in the meat industry put on so much weight within only a few weeks that by the time they are slaughtered many of them can already no longer walk. A local animal sanctuary where I live needs to keep their rescued pigs on an extremely strict diet for the same reason. These animals need to be medicated for joint problems and more often than not put down way ahead of their natural life expectancy anyway. We created a world of overtly obese animals. We created freaks of nature for our commercial benefits. That is not to say that these animals cannot live a more or less happy life if given the chance. The rescued animals I visit in the sanctuary thrive under the care they receive, by their newfound liberties. They happily enjoy their space to roam around freely, rather than being confined in tiny spaces with hundreds or thousands of fellow animals. But they are at a point where they depend on us. Just like the other animals that we like to take care of so much after we bred them to a point of no recognition: dogs. Maybe you have understood from these lines already that I and probably every vegan is or should be against most commercial breeding practices. Many dog species we created (again purely for our own selfish interests) suffer greatly from the consequences of our playing God. Shortness of breath, spine issues, joint issues, infections from skin flaps, you name it. Yes, those sausage dogs are cute on Instagram, but please do me a favor and don't buy one from a breeder. There are literally thousands of dogs waiting in shelters for a new home, so before we create more and reward unethical breeding practices with our dollar bills, please give one of those a home. The same goes for cats of course. Adopt, don't shop! But I'm digressing, I was talking about cows and pigs before. Of course one simple solution that will keep them from going extinct is doing exactly the same thing that we are doing with other animals that depend on us – we keep them as pets. There is no reason why a farmer specialized in vegetables or grains could not keep a cow or two grazing around the farm. No one said you HAVE TO kill them and eat them or milk them. You also don't milk your cat and still put in all the efforts to keep her around, right? If farmers were honest in the statements they make on all these TV segments when killings of animals is discussed, you know, when they go "oh we love our animals, we give them names, it's always a very sad day when we have to let them go," then they simply would stop doing it! You're not sending them off to college, you send them to a slaughterhouse, it's not in their interest, it's in yours. So let me quote the Black Eyed Peas and ask you, dear farmer, "where is the love?"

It is definitely true though that we would have a significant reduction in this world of cows and pigs, chickens and turkeys, and so forth. But that's also ok. There is no inherent value in billions of chickens on this planet. The opposite is the case. It only causes problems, from viral outbreaks to antibiotic resistance, to methane emissions, to polluted rivers, to deforestation and wild habitat loss. This whole argument that sometimes is made that we could not all go vegan because then all the cows would go extinct or millions of animals would die because of vegans is simply absurd. That argument suggests that you care about these animals living and existing, but you clearly don't if you currently partake in eating them. So yes, I would prefer if a pig was not even born instead of coming into this world only to get its tail chopped off, to be crammed into confinement where it can barely move, to stand in its own filth for a few months and then to get killed for no other reason than some people's drug-like addiction to bacon. And the few who will be born, actually get to live a decent life. Obviously, it would never happen anyway that the whole world went vegan in a day. When people tell you "what are we going to do with all these animals if we all went vegan tomorrow" they create the same hypothetical argument like when they send you to remote islands with nothing but a pig as a companion. It's an unrealistic scenario that somehow should justify the very realistic status quo. I usually like to offer a simple pact. "You" are allowed to eat all the currently existing cows and pigs and chickens, but not produce any more of them afterwards. I mean, they will be eaten in the real world anyway, so they might as well get eaten in your bullcrap fantasy, right? Simple deal: eat what's left, then go vegan. That's anyway how I recommend you approach your "going vegan," but more about that in the next chapter.

Probably you also have heard how the meat and dairy industry justifies its existence with the claim that a lot of land is not suitable for farming, thus making cows an indispensable asset in our fight to feed the world as they turn meadows into calories. After all, also vegans cannot digest grass, even if most vegan jokes center around the idea that we do. Of course the whole idea of having a cow around that will eat all the grass next to your house and then provide much-needed nutrition when winter hits hard has been a lifesaver for many people back in the days, before supermarkets sprouted up like mushrooms. It still may be a logic that applies to remote rural communities in underdeveloped nations. But that's not an argument for people reading books about veganism. You clearly live in a different world. And that world is producing already more food than is needed to feed everyone, only fails to distribute it fairly. And this same world could produce even more food if we didn't feed all those grains and soybeans to cows but to humans directly. So yes, there will be some pastures that will remain unused for commercial farming, but that's perfect! We are losing wildlife habitats by the second, the diversity of species is diminishing drastically, we are literally destroying the planet we live on, so what better thing could we do than give some meadows back to nature, letting forests extend again, grass to grow high and wild?

We have it in our own hands to turn this world into a fairer, less violent and more inhabitable place for everyone, not just the animals. A world without large scale animal farming would be a world with a significantly reduced pandemic risk, and if there's one thing everybody should be able to agree on, then it's that we do not want to relive the past few years – especially given that the next pandemic could turn out even much worse.

7 Just do it

When I got interested in the topics of sustainable, healthy and ethical production and consumption of food – not veganism per se, but what would eventually lead me down that path – books and documentaries were my ticket to a new world. Most of these books opened up my mind to philosophical thinking. They taught me about abhorring industry practices I was not even remotely aware of. They also sharpen my conviction that eating animals was no longer an option for me. But what disappointed me in more than one of these books was the conclusion. If an author spends hundreds of pages explaining to me how food production systems involving animals are cruel and that therefore the ethical thing to do would be to no longer partake in these wrongdoings, I kind of expect an ending along the lines of "now let's all go vegan!" Instead, they give you the sugarcoating and say something like "I probably won't be living 100% vegan from here onwards, but I learned the importance of respecting food, blah, blah and more blah." The same is true for many environmental documentaries by the way, where they will tell you for two hours that we are all doomed unless we make significant changes and then recommend you to stop using plastic straws. I get it, it's a way to reach a wider audience that is not willing to take the big step and many small steps are sometimes also a big step in the right direction. But I can't and I won't. I cannot write about all the things you just read up until here and then tell you it's ok to eat meat just on Sundays, to leave you with the illusion that if you stop using plastic straws the oceans will be clean again. I am straightforward with you and ask you, or rather kindly but pleadingly urge you to go vegan! It is now easier than ever, so if not now, when? If not you, who?

We cannot wait for politics to change the world or hope that the industries will regulate themselves. I know it's overwhelming to be confronted with different struggles and problems in this world every day. We are asked to care about the environment, donate money for starving children, sign petitions to save endangered animals, and your local politicians will do their best to highlight all the problems in your community so that they can present themselves as the solution to a better future and get your vote. But it is also important to be aware of the simplicity and power that lies in the concept of veganism. Is it a solution for all the world's problems? No. Is it perfect? No. But while it may be very difficult for the average person to directly do much about starving children at the other end of the world, it is incredibly powerful to "vote" with your dollars every meal you eat, every pair of clothing you buy, every ticket to a show you buy, etc. A single dinner with only 6 small chicken wings on your plate is already the life of 3 individual birds that you can spare! Besides, you ARE doing ~~something~~ a lot for the environment at the same time, you ARE doing something about a better future on this planet for everyone at the same time! We cannot expect politics to save us all. Politics is slow, biased by personal interests and usually short-sighted. Many government agencies give out recommendations that we should lower our consumption of meat from a health perspective. They tell you that it would be better for the planet if we favored a more plant-based diet. And then they turn around and subsidize the local meat and dairy production heavily with tax money for economic considerations. In 2020 the European Union alone spent around 100 million Euros for "market measures" of the meat, dairy and egg sector, which is still far less than the billions they spend on direct payments to keep farming profitable.[59] There are too many interests at play. And industries are unfortunately not going to change themselves, there is no regulation without public demand. As long as we don't ask for sustainable options that do not involve suffering and death, the meat industry will not suddenly wake up one day and say "how about we all start making tofu now?" There is a popular quote that is often mistakenly attributed to Gandhi but is insightful no matter where it originated: "First they ignore you, then they laugh at you, then they fight you, then you win."[60] We've already made it way past the first two stages in many areas, as it becomes more and more apparent how protective some of these industry representatives get. Legal battles have been launched by the meat and dairy industry about naming conventions of plant-based alternatives.[61] All masked behind an alleged interest in protecting consumers from unintentionally buying the wrong thing. Apparently, the milk industry is seriously concerned that we will grab a carton of soy "milk" in the supermarket and end up incredibly puzzled once we realize that no cow produce is pouring out of it at home. The meat industry would prefer if you called that vegan burger a veggie disc, just to protect you from wrongly assuming that "vegan" could be French for "beef." After all, we do switch off our brains once we read the term "burger" on a package. All joking aside, these are obviously desperate, legal attempts to slow down the spread of all these plant-based alternatives taking over supermarket shelves. Somehow nobody cared for decades that coconut milk does not derive from cows and I don't recall the last lawsuit when somebody mistakenly poured coconut milk into their cereals and died from coconut allergy. It is safe to say that we have already gotten pretty far when "they fight you" and no longer ignore you. And we know what follows after that: we must be on the verge of victory! So don't wait for politics or some kind of magic self-regulation to be happening, be the change that this world needs today. Be part of a positive movement that chooses kindness and compassion over death and destruction every single day. In other words, just do it!

....BUT! Please be smart about it. There are more than enough people on social media that heard veganism was the latest trend, jumped on the bandwagon, lived from nothing but green smoothies and then disappointedly shared with the world that a vegan diet was just not working for them. So let me be clear. It is easy being a vegan in the sense that you don't need to be a rocket scientist to become a vegan. You no longer need to go to the remotest health food shop to find a simple block of tofu. Manufacturers of all kinds of things from fashion brands to cosmetics are certifying their products as vegan-friendly left and right. You definitely don't have a lack of choice in this day and age to support you on your new journey. The internet is full of interest groups to help you find restaurants and whatever else you are on the lookout for. But it is not so easy being a vegan in the sense that you cannot just wake up tomorrow morning, remove all animal ingredients from your fridge and think that you can now just thrive on eating nothing but salads. Please do learn just the bare minimum of what kind of nutrition can be found in what type of food categories and what it means to eat a balanced diet. Eating is an essential part of our daily lives, so it should not be too much work to spend an hour or two on the website of your local vegan support group and look at some advice on how to eat well. We've become so disconnected with food that I'm convinced a bit of interest in this topic will do you good no matter what diet you end up choosing for yourself. Don't get me wrong, I'm not telling you here that you need to be a health food junkie – be my guest and eat as many fries and vegan burgers as you like, that's up to you! Just do consider that a bare minimum of balanced nutrient intake is necessary if you intend not to develop any deficiencies. I am not a doctor, so don't quote me on this (and don't sue me either – my advice is not professional), but do look at least into recommendations on vitamin B12 supplementation. Maybe also consider a medical checkup and a blood test after your first year to see how you are doing.

Another way to be smart about it is to do things at your own pace. Don't be a procrastinator though and tell me in a decade from now that you're trying to go vegan "at your own pace." But it is ok not to go cold ~~turkey~~ tofu overnight and to remove items one at a time if necessary. That is arguably even an imperative if you already own these items. Obviously, the switch to veganism should not result in you throwing stuff away. If you already own the leather jacket, keep wearing it (unless the idea of cow skin suddenly grosses you out). Once it's worn out, you can replace it with a vegan jacket. Or maybe one of your friends will be happy to receive it second hand from you and when you have "the talk", there will be something in it for them, so it's a win-win! Personally, I made an overnight switch with food and gradually removed all other items around me. My very last pair of leather sneakers is in fact still in a bag somewhere in the basement, (possibly covered in mold), just because I have not gotten myself to throw away this reminder of my younger self and "good old times," even if I clearly no longer have any use for them. A common advice is to take it one day at a time. Don't tell yourself "from today I will never eat any meat again," but rather "today I don't eat meat". Then tomorrow you do the same. And after a few days or weeks it will start being already normal because you gradually started creating new patterns in your life. Also my "overnight switch" was not intended for life. I had a week for myself alone at home and decided not to consume animal products for that time. And by the end of the week, I just continued.

Do I feel like I ever had to give up on anything? To be perfectly honest, yes. I mean, how could you not? I would be lying to you if I claimed here that I never had a moment in all these years where I was confronted with a food item or dish that I used to eat, now no longer choose to eat and didn't crave it. But not for a second did that question my choice or even tempt me to "cheat" on my principles. Unless you grow up as a vegan, you will inevitably have made non-vegan experiences that are saved in your brain and will evoke memories for the rest of your life. Maybe you smell something that takes you back to your childhood, maybe there's a specific dish that you associate with comforting moments with your family or maybe it's something as simple as a particular candy you like. And that can be challenging, I get it. That is also the reason why you cannot be TOLD to go vegan but need to DECIDE to go vegan. You need to make the connection yourself and decide for yourself that this is what you want to do because you think it's the right thing to do. Then you will endure the challenges. Then days will become months and months will become years and your new lifestyle will be nothing but normal. You will quickly learn to imitate those favorite dishes of yours if you choose to do so. But even more importantly, you will get to know tons of new things that you haven't known before, so in the aftermath, it's really more enriching than limiting. At least that's how I see it. When I look back at the foods I used to eat and the diversity of dishes I am familiar with now, veganism has added way more than it subtracted from my plates, resulting in a net gain.

I wanted to end now with a cheesy moral encouragement, telling you that also mentally (I want to avoid spiritually) you will feel so much better knowing you are making positive choices every day. But then I reflected on my own feelings and have to qualify that a bit. If I think back to my childhood, when walking past some grazing sheep, my almost instinctive move was always pulling out some grass from the sidewalk and holding it their way, hoping they would come closer and eat my offering. It was an act of curiosity, an act of kindness, an act of awe, a genuine, childlike connection with creatures that seemed not very different from our dog at home. Now, whenever I get the chance to be close enough to an animal that I know is destined for human consumption in any shape or form, I feel sad and want to apologize to them. It's hard to not think of their destiny, so sometimes ignorance is probably bliss. But I do have a newfound connection with nature and the animal kingdom that is based on respect. I no longer needlessly bat at a fly if I can easily trap it and bring it outside. Are they still annoying? Of course, but I no longer consider that a good enough reason to kill them. Even spiders, despite my arachnophobia, are no longer destined for death in my house. It takes a lot of bravery from my side, but they are actually easy to catch with a glass and a piece of cardboard. And feeding a chicken or petting a pig at a sanctuary? Well, that is simply the best experience in the world when you know that they are living a life of freedom and you can look them in the eyes knowing that you will not be eating one of their relatives later for dinner.

Understanding Vegans

8 Counting on the next generation

I remember going fishing three times as a kid. The first time was intended as an adventurous day with my uncle, where the whole point was not so much the act of fishing per se, but an outdoorsy family activity to keep a young boy entertained. Today, I obviously disagree with the idea that we teach children that killing animals is a fun way to spend your free time, but I guess you got that by now. The second time we were on a family vacation, cruising down a canal in France on a houseboat, when my cousins and I, probably out of boredom, decided to fish. As we were clearly not well prepared for that spontaneous idea, my older cousins got the more proper equipment that was available and I, as the youngest of the group, ended up with a hook on a string that I simply held down into the water. To everyone's surprise – also none of the adults expected any fruition from our attempts at "fishing" – I was the one who suddenly had a fish on the hook. Nobody really knew what to do with the poor thing, so after a bit of shouting and yelling, one of the adults unhooked the fish and released it into the water. The third time I was a little bit older, maybe 10 or 12, and I actually somehow intended to go fishing in order to eat the catch afterwards. I did not even particularly like to eat fish so much, it was more a romanticized idea, I guess. There was this tiny pond, where they artificially release trout every year that can then be fished out and paid for by weight. A very weird practice, but technically not very different from what we do with all the other animals we eat. What happened was basically that you released the hook into the water and a few seconds later there was a fish biting. Very little effort needed in terms of patience, but then again you don't get extra credit just because you had to sit around three hours for your prey to bite. My parents instructed me that as soon as I had the fish out of the water, I should hit it hard behind its head with a stick to break its neck and kill it without much suffering. I also remember that while my mom was trying to normalize the action (like, this is what you have to do if you want to eat it), my dad was a bit disgusted by the violent act (but probably less motivated by the end goal, as he doesn't like fish anyway) – both perfectly human reactions to what was going on. *Thump* and the fish no longer moved. I remember that my own emotions were somewhere caught in between the two reactions from my parents, but as I wanted to do this in the first place, I also told myself that this was what needed to be done.

In hindsight, this moment reveals so much about how we feel as a society towards the killing of animals. Almost nobody truly wants to do it. Many people say they could never kill an animal or even admit that they would not eat them if they had to do the killing themselves. Hence the popular quote that many more people would go vegetarian if slaughterhouses had glass walls. Kids identify with animals maybe even more. Again, nobody wants Bambi to be an orphan. If there is a pet around the house, most kids consider it to be their best friend. Yet, most parents teach their kids exactly what they have been taught, namely that it's ok to hurt them. Not directly, of course. We all say "go careful now" or "be gentle" when a toddler approaches a cat or a dog, but we simply ignore that what ends up on our dinner plates does not end up there by being gentle to animals. That fluffy, cute bunny needs to die for us to eat meat, it's that simple. Yet we hide the truth from our children, in fact, even from ourselves. Many people not only refuse for their kids to see video footage of what is happening in slaughterhouses, but they also don't want to see it themselves. But that's exactly what we need to do, we need to be honest. Honest to ourselves, honest to the ones we raise and teach. If it's too brutal to see, maybe it should simply not be done and is wrong in the first place? If it shouldn't be done and if we can't do it ourselves, maybe we should not support it with our dollars?

Vegan parents face a whole other level of social pressure and scrutiny because they not only made an "extreme" choice for themselves but also "force" this choice upon their children. But let's face it, every parent decides what they think is in the best interest of their children until they are old enough to make educated choices themselves. Just because your "choice" to feed dead animals to your child is in accordance with what the majority of society does, doesn't make it less of a choice you make FOR your child. Or are you suggesting that if you put a chicken in front of a toddler it would intuitively try to kill and eat it? So what is wrong with using the less violent choice as a default and then letting your kid decide when they are old enough if they prefer to kill animals in order to eat dinner or not? How come nobody has any issues with parents feeding their children group 1 carcinogenic food (processed meat)?[62] Imagine a world in which parents who raise their kids as non-smokers are stigmatized for forcing their beliefs on them. Crazy, right?

On a more optimistic note, I have the impression that teenagers and young adults these days are already much more open to the idea of veganism than previous generations. It is not all that surprising, given the amount of information that is available at their fingertips. The connection between our food choices and the state of our planet is becoming harder and harder to ignore. Thanks to modern technology, images of factory farms, slaughterhouses and animal abuse can reach millions of people within no time, making it harder and harder to look away. Veganism is simply an educated choice. If you see and understand that animals are suffering when we raise and kill them for food, if you understand that nowadays we have alternative food options and do not rely on steak for survival anymore, then where is the justification to eat animals?

Nobel prize winner Max Planck once said that scientific progress is not made by convincing opponents but rather by generational change.[63] So while the current generation is still busy filling the comment sections of articles mentioning veganism with juvenile spite like "now I'm gonna go make myself a nice, juicy steak," I do have a lot of faith in the next generation. A generation that grows up in a world where supermarkets stocked with all kinds of alternatives to meat, dairy, eggs and seafood are the norm. Outdated views will die out because the next generation grows up in a world where more and more restaurants offer so much tasty vegan food and ordering a vegan option is no longer a stigmatized special request but simply a regular order. They grow up in a world where fashion manufacturers no longer work with leather and fur. A world where animal-based ingredients become the exception rather than the vegan alternative. This will be the generation that has it easier than it has ever been to make a positive choice and leave animal-based products behind in the past, making it nothing but a horrific chapter in our history on this planet. Yes, there is a long way to go, but I do have hope. The path is prepared, the doors have been opened and we just need to step through. The future that I envision is near and that future is vegan.

Sources

[1] M. Pollan. 2006. *The Omnivore's Dilemma*. Bloomsbury London.
[2] K. Duve. 2011. *Anständig Essen*. Galiani Berlin. 85-86.
[3] Britannica, The Editors of Encyclopaedia. "*vegetarianism*". Encyclopedia Britannica, 11 Aug. 2020, https://www.britannica.com/topic/vegetarianism.
[4] D. Watson. 1944. *The Vegan News – Quarterly Magazine of the non-dairy vegetarians*. PDF Scan obtained via http://www.abolitionistapproach.com/wp-content/uploads/2015/09/vegan_news_1.pdf
[5] The Vegan Society. 2022. https://www.vegansociety.com/about-us/history
[6] *Veganism*. 2022. Wikipedia, The Free Encyclopedia. https://en.wikipedia.org/wiki/Veganism
[7] L. Ruehlman et al. 2022. Adherence versus striving to adhere to vegan, vegetarian, or pescetarian diets: Applying a goal-centered, self-regulatory framework. *Journal of health psychology* 27 (9): 2236-2246.
[8] Vegan Chronicles. 23.12.2016. *F.A.Q. Vegan*. https://www.facebook.com/veganchronicles/photos/a.623109541099214/1253241998085962
[9] Swissmilk. 2022. *Plant based: was heisst «pflanzenbasierte Ernährung»?* https://www.swissmilk.ch/de/ernaehrung/pflanzenbasiert-essen/plant-based-was-heisst-pflanzenbasierte-ernaehrung/

[10] *Vegetarianism by country.* 2022. Wikipedia, The Free Encyclopedia. https://en.wikipedia.org/wiki/Vegetarianism_by_country

[11] K. Modlinska et al. 2020. Gender Differences in Attitudes to Vegans/Vegetarians and Their Food Preferences, and Their Implications for Promoting Sustainable Dietary Patterns - A Systematic Review. *Sustainability* 6292 (12). Doi:103390/su12166292.

[12] A. Mood and P. Brooke. 2010. *Estimating the Number of Fish Caught in Global Fishing Each Year.* http://fishcount.org.uk/published/std/fishcountstudy.pdf

[13] H. Ritchie and M. Roser. 2021. "*Biodiversity*". https://ourworldindata.org/fish-and-overfishing#global-fish-production

[14] C.M. Colvin and L. Marino. 2015. Signs of Intelligent Life. *Natural History.* https://www.naturalhistorymag.com/features/122899/signs-of-intelligent-life

[15] FAO STAT (United Nations) – *Aggregated Livestock Numbers 2019* http://fao.org/faostat/en/#data

[16] W.J. Craig and A.R. Mangels. 2009. Position of the American Dietetic Association: vegetarian diets. *Journal of the American Dietetic Association* 109 (7): 1266-1282.

[17] Nation Earth. 2005. *Earthlings.* www.earthlings.com

[18] T. Laeenaert. 2017. *How to Create a Vegan World – A Pragmatic Approach.* New York, Lantern Books.

[19] L. Johnson. 2015. The Religion of Ethical Veganism. *Journal of Animal Ethics* 1 (5): 31-68.

[20] M. Joy. 2009. *Why We Love Dogs, Eat Pigs, and Wear Cows: An Introduction to Carnism.* Conari Press.

[21] M-L. Augère-Granier. 2019. *The EU Poultry meat and egg sector – main features, challenges and prospects.* European Parliamentary Research Service. https://www.europarl.europa.eu/RegData/etudes/IDAN/2019/644195/EPRS_IDA(2019)644195_EN.pdf

[22] ADAS UK Ltd. 2016. *Comparison of the Regulatory Framework and Key Practices in the Poultry Meat Supply Chain in the EU and USA*. https://britishpoultry.org.uk/identity-cms/wp-content/uploads/2018/05/2016-ADAS-EU-US-comparison.pdf

[23] FAO. *Gateway to poultry production and products*. https://www.fao.org/poultry-production-products/production/poultry-species/chickens/en/

[24] FAO STAT (United Nations) – *Aggregated Livestock Numbers 2020. Eggs, hen, in shell*. http://fao.org/faostat/en/#data

[25] F. Street. 2018. *Switzerland bans boiling lobsters alive*. CNN Travel. https://edition.cnn.com/travel/article/switzerland-lobster-boiling-banned/index.html

[26] J. Geldmann and J.P. Gonzalez-Varo. 2018. Conserving honey bees does not help wildlife. *Science* 6374 (359): 392-393. DOI: 10.1126/science.aar2269

[27] E. Visontay. 2020. *Nike and Puma flouting California ban on selling kangaroo leather goods, animal rights group claims*. https://www.theguardian.com/australia-news/2020/aug/01/nike-and-puma-flouting-california-ban-on-selling-kangaroo-leather-goods-animal-rights-group-claims

[28] A. Weissman. 2016. *Is your leather from China? It might be made of dog or cat skin*. The Guardian. https://www.theguardian.com/business/2016/jul/31/dog-cat-leather-china-us-congress-trade-peta

[29] The Guardian. 2008. *Don't hide from the truth*. https://www.theguardian.com/lifeandstyle/2008/aug/27/ethicalfashion.leather

[30] R. Egglestone. 2021. *Silk-Making is an Ancient Practice That Presents an Ethical Dilemma*. Discover Magazine. https://www.discovermagazine.com/planet-earth/silk-making-is-an-ancient-practice-that-presents-an-ethical-dilemma

[31] MSPCA-Angell. *Circus Animal Welfare*. https://www.mspca.org/animal_protection/circus-animal-welfare/

[32] Animal Ethics. *Circuses and other shows.* https://www.animal-ethics.org/circuses-shows/

[33] C. Redmond. 2017. *A Study of the Conservation Status of Species Held in Welsh Zoos.* Freedom for Animals. https://www.freedomforanimals.org.uk/Handlers/Download.ashx?IDMF=05d25153-9e83-4b3e-8c0c-71278e9044ca

[34] Earthling Ed. 2021. *Why SHOULDN'T we support zoos and their conservation work?* YouTube. https://www.youtube.com/watch?v=p3l87NywToQ

[35] A. Akhtar. 2015. The flaws and human harms of animal experimentation. *Cambridge Quarterly of Healthcare Ethics.* 24 (4): 407-419. https://www.ncbi.nlm.nih.gov/pmc/articles/PMC4594046/

[36] J. Langel. 2022. *Is Humane-Washing of Meat and Poultry False Advertising?* The Langel Firm. https://www.thelangelfirm.com/debt-collection-defense-blog/2022/june/the-ugly-truths-about-humane-washing-of-meat-pro/

[37] WHO European Office for the Prevention and Control of Noncommunicable Diseases. 2021. *Plant-based diets and their impact on health, sustainability and the environment: a review of evidence.* WHO Regional Office for Europe. https://apps.who.int/iris/bitstream/handle/10665/349086/WHO-EURO-2021-4007-43766-61591-eng.pdf

[38] Harvard T.H. Chan School of Public Health. 2015. *WHO report says eating processed meat is carcinogenic: Undersatnding the findings.* https://www.hsph.harvard.edu/nutritionsource/2015/11/03/report-says-eating-processed-meat-is-carcinogenic-understanding-the-findings/

[39] H. Ritchie and M. Roser. 2020. *Emissions by sector.* Our World in Data. https://ourworldindata.org/emissions-by-sector

[40] D. Carrington. 2018. *Avoiding meat and dairy is 'single biggest way' to reduce your impact on Earth.* The Guardian. https://www.theguardian.com/environment/2018/may/31/

avoiding-meat-and-dairy-is-single-biggest-way-to-reduce-your-impact-on-earth

[41] H. Ritchie. 2020. *You want to reduce the carbon footprint of your food? Focus on what you eat, not whether your food is local.* Our World in Data. https://ourworldindata.org/food-choice-vs-eating-local

[42] H. Ritchie. 2021. *Cutting down forests: what are the drivers of deforestation?* Our World in Data. https://ourworldindata.org/what-are-drivers-deforestation

[43] W. A. Barr et al. 2022. *No sustained increase in zooarchaeological evidence for carnivory after the appearance of Homo erectus.* PNAS 119 (5). https://www.pnas.org/doi/10.1073/pnas.2115540119

[44] Cleveland Clinic. 2019. *Do I Need to Worry About Eating 'Complete' Proteins?* Health Essentials. https://health.clevelandclinic.org/do-i-need-to-worry-about-eating-complete-proteins/

[45] H. Ritchie. 2020. *You want to reduce the carbon footprint of your food? Focus on what you eat, not whether your food is local.* Our World in Data. https://ourworldindata.org/food-choice-vs-eating-local

[46] H. Ritchie and M. Roser. 2020. *Environmental Impacts of Food Production.* Our World in Data. https://ourworldindata.org/environmental-impacts-of-food

[47] W. Fraanje and T. Garnett. 2020. *Soy: food, feed, and land use change.* Tabledebates.org. https://www.tabledebates.org/building-blocks/soy-food-feed-and-land-use-change

[48] WHO. 2016. *Health topics: Obesity.* https://www.who.int/health-topics/obesity

[49] W.J. Craig and A.R. Mangels. 2009. Position of the American Dietetic Association: vegetarian diets. *Journal of the American Dietetic Association* 109 (7): 1266-1282.

[50] A. Wasley, C. D. Cook and N. Jones. 2018. *Two amputations a week: the cost of working in a US meat plant.* The Guardian. https://www.theguardian.com/environment/2018/jul/05/amputations-serious-injuries-us-meat-industry-plant

[51] J. Slade and E. Alleyne. 2021. *The Psychological Impact of Slaughterhouse Employment: A Systematic Literature Review.* Trauma, Violence, & Abuse. https://journals.sagepub.com/doi/full/10.1177/15248380211030243

[52] FAO. 2022. *Antimicrobial Resistance: What is it?* https://www.fao.org/antimicrobial-resistance/background/what-is-it/en/

[53] WHO. 2020. *Zoonoses.* https://www.who.int/news-room/fact-sheets/detail/zoonoses

[54] I. Binnie. 2015. *Italy hunts for solution to wild boar emergency.* Reuters. https://www.reuters.com/article/us-italy-boar-idUSKCN0SU1JN20151105

[55] N.H. Lents. 2018. *The Evolutionay Quirk That Made Vitamin B12 Part of Our Diet.* Discover Magazine. https://www.discovermagazine.com/health/the-evolutionary-quirk-that-made-vitamin-b12-part-of-our-diet

[56] Animal Protection Index. 2020. http://api.worldanimalprotection.org

[57] E. Winters. 2022. *This is vegan propaganda (and other lies the meat industry tells you).* London, Vermilion.

[58] A. Shepon, G. Eshel, E. Noor and R. Milo. 2018. The opportunity cost of animal based diets exceeds all food losses. *Proceedings of the National Academy of Sciences* 115 (15): 3804-3809. https://www.pnas.org/content/115/15/3804

[59] European Union. 2021. *Statistical Factsheet.* https://ec.europa.eu/info/sites/default/files/food-farming-fisheries/farming/documents/agri-statistical-factsheet-eu_en.pdf

[60] AP. 2018. *Quote wrongly attributed to Mahatma Gandhi.* https://apnews.com/article/archive-fact-checking-2315880316

[61] I. Kwai. 2020. *E.U. Says Veggie Burgers Can Keep Their Name.* New York Times. https://www.nytimes.com/2020/10/23/world/europe/eu-plant-based-labeling.html

[62] WHO Team. 2015. *Cancer: Carcinogenicity of the consumption of red meat and processed meat.* https://www.who.int/news-

room/questions-and-answers/item/cancer-carcinogenicity-of-the-consumption-of-red-meat-and-processed-meat

[63] N. Sam. 2013. Planck's Principle. *PsychologyDictionary.org*. https://psychologydictionary.org/plancks-principle

Printed in Great Britain
by Amazon